ADVANCE PRAISE FOR
WORLD WITHOUT END

"In these penetrating and beautifully wrought essays, Martha Park employs her many identities—artist, naturalist, southerner, mother, preacher's daughter astray—to investigate profound questions about faith and the fate of our planet. It is rare to find a voice like this: at once vulnerable and rigorous, skeptical and compassionate, commanding and humble in the presence of mystery. It is rarer still when that voice—its questions and ideas—are so vividly embodied, so intimately involved with the sensory world. I have been raving about this book since I finished reading its exquisite and devastating final lines. As the title suggests, I suspect *World Without End* will endure long past the season of its birth, moving and engaging readers for years to come."

LISA WELLS,
author of *Believers: Making a Life at the End of the World*

"It's hard to imagine a more trustworthy guide through the terrain of faith and doubt in this era of ecological catastrophe than Martha Park. In her hands, the stories we tell ourselves about the world—and how it may or may not end—are forces of nature in and of themselves, animated by electricity, gravity, and wonder. Like the theologian Martin Buber, Park sees the 'paradoxical unity of what one might typically see as opposites': not only on the grand scale of embodiment and limitlessness, time and eternity; but also in the messy details that emerge when family or community members are polarized by political or religious beliefs. Park's illustrations, like her writing, are clear-eyed, carefully observed, fully of this world, yet mysteriously transcendent. This is a book to treasure."

ARWEN DONAHUE
author of *Landings: A Crooked Creek Farm Year*

"In elegant and exacting prose, Martha Park draws readers into the white southern Christianity of preppers and young earth creationists—but also of her progressive, renegade pastor-father. Compassionate but unflinching, Park shows us what faith can do when practiced with empathy instead of fear. An important new voice, and *World Without End* is a much needed reckoning."

CAMERON DEZEN HAMMON
author of *This Is My Body: A Memoir of Religious and Romantic Obsession*

"Rarely have I tucked in so hungrily to an essay collection, felt so welcomed. These pieces, beautifully connected to one another yet wide-reaching in terms of idea and question and observation, are held gently in their places by Martha Park's tender illustrations and vulnerability. Weeks on, I still haven't stopped thinking about it."

ELLA FRANCES SANDERS
author of *Everything, Beautiful: A Guide to Finding Hidden Beauty in the World*

"This is an extraordinary collection on doubt, faith, climate, community, fear, entanglement, awe, and the essential things we owe one another. I'm deeply grateful for these essays, which are both precise and searching, enormously intimate and rigorously reported."

MOLLY MCCULLY BROWN
author of *Places I've Taken My Body*

WORLD WITHOUT END

WORLD WITHOUT END

MARTHA PARK

HUB CITY PRESS
SPARTANBURG, SC

Executive Director, Publisher: Meg Reid
Managing Editor: Kate McMullen
Marketing Assistant: Julie Jarema
Editor: Katherine Webb-Hehn
Copy Editors: Iza Wojciechowska, Melissa Thorpe
Author Photo: Katie Barber
Book Design Lead: Meg Reid

Essays in this collection have previously appeared in *Orion Magazine* ("Natural Ends"), *Guernica* ("World Without End"), *The Bitter Southerner* ("This is Paradise," "The Ark at the End of the World," "TV Apocalypse" as "The Life I Have"), *Image Journal* ("The Charged World," "Crying in Church"), and *The Louisville Review* ("Arkansas Prophecy").

Library of Congress Cataloging-in-Publication Data

Names: Park, Martha, 1988- author, illustrator.
Title: World without end : essays on apocalypse and after / Martha Park.
Description: Spartanburg, SC : Hub City Press, [2025]
Identifiers: LCCN 2024052419 (print)
LCCN 2024052420 (ebook)
ISBN 9798885740487 (hardback)
ISBN 9798885740531 (epub)
Subjects: LCSH: Park, Martha, 1988-
Park, Martha, 1988—Religion.
Women authors, AmericanBiography.
Children of clergy–United States–Biography.
Climatic changes–Social aspects–Southern States.
Climatic changes–Religious aspects–Christianity.
Southern States–Biography.
Classification:
LCC PS3616.A74355 Z46 2025 (print)
LCC PS3616.A74355 (ebook)
DDC 814.6--dc23/eng/20250203
LC record available at
https://lccn.loc.gov/2024052419
LC ebook record available at
https://lccn.loc.gov/2024052420

First edition | Printed in the USA

HUB CITY PRESS
153 North Spring Street
Spartanburg, SC 29306
864.577.9349 | www.hubcity.org

for James and Juniper, new worlds.

and still the breath of God comes back
from the time that isn't over yet.

Maurice Manning, *One Man's Dark*

TABLE OF CONTENTS

THE CHARGED WORLD

WHEN MY FATHER FINISHED seminary, he served his first small church in Beech Bluff, Tennessee. It was 1981 or 1982. He was single and drove a little moped, took disco dancing lessons to stave off loneliness, and survived on church ladies' casseroles. He was working as a counselor at a church summer camp when he got a phone call: Five boys, members of his congregation, had been rolling a grain auger across dewy open pastures and pushed too close to a live wire. They didn't even touch it, only came close enough for the electric charge to jump from the wire to the metal of the grain auger. Three were electrocuted and died instantly; the other two were seriously hurt.

One of the dead boys and one of the living were brothers. The surviving brother was still unconscious in the hospital when my father left camp and drove the hour back to Beech Bluff to see Catherine, the boys' mother. My father was twenty-six or twenty-seven then. During college he'd watched his father die, and in seminary he took classes on death and pastoral care, but he did not feel particularly prepared to encounter this grieving mother or her pain.

Riding his moped down winding back roads toward her house, he tried to drum up words that could offer comfort beyond his own understanding. Catherine's house sat just across the street from the field where the accident happened. From her driveway, my father could see the grain auger, the drooping power line, the muddy ambulance tire tracks drying in the heat of the day, the patches of grass still flattened from the weight of the boys' bodies. He took off his helmet and knocked on her door.

I heard the story of the electrocuted boys many times growing up. When my father first told it to me, he might have meant it as a practical lesson, a warning about the dangers of water and electricity. But this was around the same time that he was reading me Bible stories at bedtime, and I stored the electrocuted boys away in the part of my brain where shepherd boys killed giants, where women were visited by angels who told them their futures, where men wrestled all night with God and were rewarded with a blessing—and a wound.

Those electrocuted boys took up a kind of mythical place in my head, and they stayed there a long time. When I was sixteen years old and shocked myself in a motel room, it was the electrocuted boys I thought of first: My hand felt suddenly fused to the outlet, I heard the electric current buzzing through my bloodstream, and wondered if those boys had heard the snap of electricity surging through their bodies before they hit the ground.

My father always told me his wiring was off: His first house was struck by lightning and burned to the ground, and once he saw a fireball burst from his television and roll across the living-room floor. I grew up believing these strange electrical occurrences had something to do with his body, as if he were an unknowing, unwilling conductor. He told me he'd passed his wiring on to me—when I was born, my black hair stood up straight like I'd stuck a fork in a socket.

On the night Memphis was struck by its worst ice storm in a hundred years, my father was on a plane flying to Israel. I was six years old, watching cartoons at the parsonage, when all the lights went out and the television screen fizzled into blackness. Coated with ice, the power lines snapped. It was the same year I'd started seeing visions: Every morning, eating cereal at the dining-room table, I saw a cross in the shiny silver of the spoon. I turned the spoon—watching the cross stretch in one direction and then the other—and believed the spoon might be a channel between heaven and earth, delivering a sacred message directly into my hands. I didn't question whether visions worked through such commonplace vessels—a scuffed spoon, my small body straining for signs.

It would be years before I realized I had been seeing the reflection of the ceiling fan in the spoon's shiny surface. It would be years before I knew electricity worked in my body, my father's body, just like anyone else's. But on the night my father flew to Israel, I didn't know that yet. So as land and oceans separated our bodies for the first time, I figured the electricity had followed him, the greater force, leaving my mother and me in a house gone dark.

When the ice storm hit and transformers started exploding one by one, my mother came running and then I was in her arms. The sky was full of electricity, and I knew my father was somewhere over the ocean far away, maybe feeling our fear, through some grace, like a spark of nervous energy in his own body.

In science class we learned about electricity by rubbing balloons against our heads. When we pulled the balloons away, our hair stretched upward, each strand reaching for the balloon's rubbery skin. The teacher explained that when two surfaces contacted and separated, and at least one of the surfaces resisted electrical current, a static electric charge was created.

That year I announced to my class that my father had been electrocuted over the weekend. I repeated his explanation: The electric current had traveled from the refrigerator through his body while he stood on an iron heating grate. He'd used the word *conductor,* which I'd always associated with music or trains. I learned the difference between two other words: "If your father is not dead," the teacher ventured, "then let's say he's been *shocked,* not electrocuted."

The teacher passed out small black magnets and we turned them this way and that, feeling the surprise pull and push of the little bars attracting and repelling each other. In my hands, the actions of these inanimate objects felt willful. When the magnets repelled each other, no matter how hard I tried to push them together, they swiveled away, unable or unwilling to make contact.

"Objects with the same charge," the teacher said, "repel each other."

This kind of phrasing troubled me. If my father and I had the same wiring, the same essential charge, would we push each other away? When I was upset with him, I wrote him long letters and slid them under my bedroom door, into the hallway. Then I'd lie on the floor, my ear pressed to the wood, listening for his footsteps to pass by my room. Sometimes, if I waited long enough there on the floor, I'd get a glimpse of his hand when he stooped to pick the paper up.

Even when I was angry at my father—*repelled,* the door shut between us—I reached for him, my folded letters tossed out into the hallway like a baited hook into a stream. A half hour or an hour later, I'd hear the scratch of folded paper as he slid his response under my bedroom door. His letters, just like his sermons, were written on yellow legal paper in his tight, leaning script.

In school we were taught that rubber shoes would keep us safe from a lightning strike. We were taught to be careful not to mix water and electricity: no hair dryers near a full bathtub, no showers during a thunderstorm. We learned that lightning is itself a kind of static spark. The teacher didn't tell us that the brightest part of the lightning flash is the return stroke, when the current of positive charge races up its own channel, back toward the thundercloud it came from.

When my father went to Israel, he traveled with a group of preachers and visited holy sites. When they reached the Jordan River all the Baptist preachers ran into the water, baptizing each other. My father sat with his fellow Methodists on the shore, eating the sandwiches they'd packed that morning, watching the Baptists dunk each other in turn. He'd always told me Methodists figure once is enough: Methodists don't re-baptize, and they don't do immersion.

But when I was in high school, in the wake of some unusual circumstances, my father agreed to baptize a group of teenagers by immersion. He contacted a large church outside town and asked to borrow their baptismal font for a few hours on a Saturday afternoon. He organized carpools and vans to shuttle his congregation out to the borrowed church. Then, a week before the planned baptism, another preacher across town waded into his own baptismal font and was electrocuted in front of his congregation when his microphone fell into the water.

I didn't want my father anywhere near pools of water and electric currents. I told him to scrap the whole thing and sprinkle water onto the kids' heads at his own church, like he'd always done before. I told him that it wasn't the water's depth that mattered, or whether it was blessed or from the bathroom sink. I told him this as if I wasn't repeating back to him everything he'd ever told me about baptism. My father eventually agreed not to use a microphone, but I went to the service and made sure there weren't any electrical cords or appliances near the font, just in case. Then I sat back in the pews and watched as my father led each of the kids into the pool.

I'd watched my father baptize dozens of babies by sprinkling a little water on their heads. But this time, I was the same age as the kids climbing in and out of the pool, and I could easily imagine joining them. I would lean back, and the water would come rushing over my face and hair. My father would help me reemerge, disoriented, feeling somehow changed.

My father didn't baptize me. Two of his old seminary buddies did it. But when I was a child he washed my hair every night. Kneeling on the cold tile, he would pour water over my head with a plastic lemonade pitcher. He would wring my hair dry, wrap me in warm towels, and put me to bed. Growing up, I thought of that ritual as our own nightly baptism. But that day, as I watched my friends climb in and out of the water, I longed for a do-over, and I had to stop myself from climbing in so he could baptize me himself. I wanted to meet him there, in that sacrament, a space that seemed a little more sacred than the prayers we said before dinner. I wanted to feel my father's hand against my forehead, the water on my skin, as he called me into God's family, his own.

When I asked my father why he didn't baptize me, he told me if I get married he won't perform my wedding ceremony, either. There are moments, he said, when he gets to be just my dad, to sit back and cry. A week before my baptism, when I was nine months old, my father wrote a letter to me and printed it in his church newsletter. He wrote, "By our example and teaching, we hope to guide you, that one day you might accept God's grace for yourself." I can imagine him, a new dad and a young pastor, writing these words and negotiating this new space, figuring out its boundaries.

The Trappist monk Thomas Merton writes that baptism imparts both an identity and a "divine vocation," because baptism distinguishes us from each other, sets each of us apart in our own relationship with God, "unknown to anyone else who has ever lived under the sun." Therefore, Merton writes, "...every sacrament of union is also a sacrament of separation."

In many ways, not just in baptism, my father has resisted serving as a conduit between me and God. The language of the concrete and the abstract, of water and electricity, seem to braid themselves together in the word *conduit,* with its three primary definitions: the first, a channel for conveying water; second, a trough or duct used to protect electric wiring; third, a means of transmitting something. My father has been all of these, whether he intended to or not. He has, through baptism, conveyed water over countless bowed heads. He has felt the snap of electric current running through his body and his home. And my father has transmitted something of his wiring to me: some leaning toward mystery, some ornery indecisiveness, some uncertain reaching toward faith.

The poet Li-Young Lee writes about his relationship to faith and his father, a Presbyterian minister. He writes that, from a genetic or hereditary perspective, his father's influence made him obsessed with spiritual matters. But according to "the Buddhist or karmic view," he writes, "in another lifetime he and I were both obsessed with this stuff, so I became his son." It's hard to imagine a different version of myself, a version that is not my father's daughter, who did not dream in parables and hymns. As I struggle to parse what is mine from what is my father's, I come back to something other than genes, other than destiny or karma. I come back to the wiring of our bodies, the electrical impulses and snapping synapses we share.

Earth's magnetic field was one of those things we learned about in school that seemed to have clearly been made up: some unseen force emanating from the earth's insides through space, created by electric currents formed deep in the earth's core, radiating at an angle according to earth's axis, and constantly changing—even reversing, in fact, every several hundred thousand years, sending the world topsy-turvy. It was one of those invisible things, the teacher said, telling us and other creatures where to go and how.

For years I seemed only to be moving apart and away, separating myself: hundreds of miles away from my parents' house and my father's churches, I felt as if there were some current directing my own course, some force running just over earth's surface—or through it—guiding and repelling and propelling me on, further.

Some animals find their way home using earth's magnetic field. In 1957, a scientist named Hans Fromme discovered the robins he kept in a cage were anxious, moving over and over again to one corner of the cage. In a windowless room, the robins were unable to feel the temperature shifting toward fall or see the sun or stars—all the things Fromme thought they needed to sense the changing seasons. Still the robins moved repeatedly into the southwest corner of their cage, following the quiet urging of the earth's own invisible force. They aren't the only ones: bacteria can use the earth's magnetic field to find their way between water and muddy banks; not long ago, researchers discovered that rainbow trout have small quantities of magnetite in their snouts, helping them align with the unseen currents of the earth's magnetic field.

At least, that's how I understood it. There are some things I have to hear over and over again to get right. I always thought of water as a conductor. But water molecules, on their own, have no charge and are unable to conduct electricity. It's the minerals present in unpurified water—like the fresh dew across which the boys rolled their grain auger—that can conduct electricity. With electricity as with baptism, it's not the water that's doing the work, but something else. To conduct electricity, water needs to be less than pure. And to mean anything at all, baptism needs something else—intention, maybe some kind of unearned grace—far more than it needs water.

In church we lived according to the liturgical calendar, the cycle of stories creating a rhythm for our weeks and years. Repetition and storytelling were how I understood the world, as I heard my father's stories over and over. They came first in the car on the way to school, or as I lay in bed waiting for sleep. Months or years later they would resurface, transformed into sermons. Between tellings, their meanings would change.

I was in my twenties when I heard my father tell the story of the electrocuted boys again, this time as a sermon. He talked about how he and Catherine, the boys' mother, had just finished up a group Bible study on the will of God. When my father arrived at her house that day, feeling so anxious and unprepared, she opened the door and took him in her arms. Before he could say anything, she told him she knew her son's death was not God's will. In that moment, my father felt the church had helped her. Looking out over his congregation, he said, "God uses the church to prepare us for the strangeness of life."

Hearing the story again as an adult, I understood that, for my father, its meaning had nothing to do with electricity or water or miracles or any of the things it had meant to me as a child. For him, the story was about the boys' mother. She knew she could not blame God for everything. She understood that we live in a world governed by hidden wiring, natural laws. She understood that the boys' deaths were an accident, not the result of God doling out fates like a dealer with a deck of cards.

The story's meaning shifted for me, too, over time, loosening itself from the specific events and gesturing outward, toward stories themselves. The stories my father told—whether from his personal life or from scripture, were slippery, changing shape depending on the form or the audience or the passage of time. They allowed me to glimpse different versions of my father and his faith as it changed, too, over the course of his life. These stories seemed to say that stories themselves have no fixed meaning. Instead they are deep wells, infinitely plumbable, that we can return to endlessly to find that somehow they—or we—have changed.

In my father's notebook, at the top of his sermon about the electrocuted boys, he wrote a single phrase: *Why I Still Go to Church.* He never addressed this question directly in the text of the sermon itself, but the question hovered at the edges: Why are we here, in this place, every Sunday morning, when we could be anywhere else in the world?

I think my father still goes to church, in part, because it's one place he can encounter the stories he's needed to hear over and over again. My father knew the boys' deaths were not God's will, but sometimes we need to hear things repeated, or from someone else's mouth. There is no single reason why I don't go to church, anymore, but surely one of them is that if I were to walk into any of the churches, in any of the towns I've lived in, my father would not be there to welcome me inside.

Five hundred miles from home, in a second-story apartment overlooking the little mountain town where I'd made my latest home, my father called while I was cooking dinner. From this vantage, looking out over my new neighborhood, I could see swallows flying in erratic formations over church steeples. I felt constantly disoriented, there, the ring of mountains on the horizon obscuring my sense of direction; if there were electromagnetic fields running through this town, they seemed to be faulty.

I was standing at the stove stirring a pot of rice when my father told me he would be retiring, years earlier than I'd expected. I had not expected it at all, not really; his leaving, or the effect it would have on me in that moment or in the coming years. I couldn't have imagined, then, the way his exit from the church would lead me on a quest of my own: to return home, to reexamine my own relationship with faith.

Outside, the day's light faded, until all I could see was my reflection in the kitchen window, standing motionless with a wooden spoon in my hand, phone pressed to my ear. As he talked, a compass whirred inside my chest, spinning in endless circles. It was a twelve-hour drive home, and I wouldn't even know which way to go, which streets to take. So I asked my father to tell me, one more time, about the day the boys were electrocuted.

The phone grew hot on my cheek as my father tunneled into the story once more, as I'd tunneled into it over and over again. As I listened to my father talk, time rewinding to the years before I was born, I ticked off the parts of the story I already knew and remembered as clearly as if I'd been there myself: the dewy field, the dangling power line, the boys thrown to the ground.

Then he said, "I bet two of those boys had their hands on the rubber tires and the other three had their hands on the metal sides. It all came down to that, where they had their hands."

I imagined my father in that farmhouse living room; his hair jet-black and tousled from the winding drive to Beech Bluff. He settles onto a floral-printed couch across from the large picture window and watches the glint of the day's last light on the side of the overturned grain auger. My father reaches out to hold the hands of the family members gathered around him. The sun withdraws from the sky. By now, the blades of grass pressed flat under the weight of the boys' bodies have righted themselves, standing up, one by one.

WORLD WITHOUT END

ON MY FIRST VISIT to my husband's childhood home in western Kentucky, after I got the tour of the house, the yard, and the garden, we paused on the deck overlooking waves of tall, undulating grasses. Colin nudged his father: "Aren't you going to show her the bunker?"

I'd been told about the bunker—a basement converted into a survivalist's dream. We walked down a flight of stairs and into a room lined with shelves of canned food, five-gallon drums of water, flashlights and walkie-talkies, shotguns and hunting rifles and crossbows, and enough home-brewed beer to ride out the world's end buzzed, surrounded by taxidermied turkeys preserved in mid-flight across the basement walls.

When we went to bed that night, I asked Colin, in a whisper, whether his dad had believed the world would end with Y2K.

"No," he said. "It's more recent than that." Above us, his childhood bedroom ceiling glowed with the light of a hundred stick-on stars. "It's kind of an Obama reelection, they're-gonna-take-our-guns, NRA Fox News–apocalypse type thing."

My husband grew up attending a nondenominational evangelical church, listening to Christian rock, and ornamenting himself in handmade hemp jewelry strung with tiny crosses. He has described to me a frequent occurrence from his youth: getting out of the shower and toweling off in the bathroom, he'd become aware of an eerie silence. Wandering the house and its empty rooms, he'd find his mother's laundry folded on the bed, his father's sandwich half-eaten on the kitchen counter, his sister vanished from the room where she had been playing, her toys scattered across her bedroom floor. In those moments, his family had usually stepped outside, or gone to the basement. But he settled on the most obvious explanation for the empty house: "They'd all been raptured," he told me, "and I'd been left behind."

Until we moved to Memphis, Colin and I lived far from our families and felt even further from the faith traditions of our childhoods. But lately, the religious beliefs we were raised with seem to be floating to the surface of our daily lives. We compare notes constantly, and find that our experiences growing up in church seem almost entirely unrelated. From my perspective as the daughter of a progressive Methodist preacher, my husband's evangelical upbringing seems an alien thing, distorted and strange. When I was growing up, I'd never even heard of the rapture, and would never have assumed an empty house meant I'd been abandoned, left behind, for God to judge or damn.

I've often wondered what effect it would have on a child—or an adult—to believe that the world as we know it was destined to be consumed in a final fiery moment sent from God. But as end-times thinking has spread beyond the walls of any specific church, the fast-approaching end of the world doesn't seem so abstract or far-fetched anymore.

Memories of my childhood growing up in my father's churches come mostly in snippets, disparate images disconnected from any sense of time other than the pattern created by Sunday mornings spent sitting in scuffed wooden pews. I remember standing on a stepstool in my father's pulpit, forgetting the words to a song mid-solo, and retreating to my mother, red-cheeked, to cry into her lap. I remember learning to play the handbells, and our teacher telling us to pretend there was a wall of ice cream in front of us, to imagine using the handbell as a scoop.

There is one memory, from one of those innumerable Sundays, that stands out with particular clarity: I was five or six years old, and my father announced from the pulpit that he would be preaching from the Book of Revelation. He asked all the children to leave, to follow our Sunday School teacher down the hall. He was worried we would be scared by the apocalyptic language of the Bible's last book—all that fire, all those beasts. I filed out with the other kids, feeling suddenly anonymous and abandoned, like my father was keeping a secret from me. We spent that Sunday making cards for all the homebound old ladies we'd never see, though we wrote their names hundreds of times on hundreds of pieces of folded cardstock.

I don't always know how to distinguish between my father's individual beliefs and the theology of his denomination. Growing up, Wesleyan values like reason, discernment, and grace hovered far above other Christian concepts—like salvation, redemption, and sin—that I didn't hear about so much. My father never preached much about any life other than this life, or any world other than this one. But the apocalypse is still a defining feature of evangelical theologies like the one my husband grew up with.

My father, like many contemporary mainline Protestant scholars, sees the Bible as a collection of texts written—and deeply revised, over the course of centuries—by people whose worldviews were necessarily constrained and influenced by their own cultural contexts.

He reads the Bible's last book not as a prediction of the world's future end, but as a coded depiction of oppression under an authoritarian empire. In this way, he would argue, the Bible's final book has even more relevance for our contemporary lives than if it were predicting the future. For my father, the Book of Revelation, as with all the books of the Bible, describes "their then," as theologian Marcus Borg phrases it, not "our now."

But for the first time, and with increasing frequency, I've found the language of apocalypse creeping up in my own life. When my husband and I moved to Memphis, and bought a small bungalow next-door to my parents and one house over from my sister and her husband, my brother-in-law began calling our combined properties *the Compound.* Gesturing to our three houses with their conjoined backyards, he joked that Colin and I would be the ones protecting the northwest side when the world ends. "We've got the eastern flank covered," he said, "and your parents have got the south side."

This kind of language didn't surprise me; I didn't even think to ask what danger, exactly, he anticipated coming our way. Lately, it seems we all—secular or religious, conservative or liberal—sense some tension that has to give, some ending on the horizon. When my friends and I commiserate about our low-paying jobs, sky-rocketing debt, and the looming doom of the climate crisis, we joke about the absurdity of planning for the future: "My retirement plans," I hear myself say, "consist entirely of assuming the world will no longer be habitable by the time I'm sixty-five."

In the months leading up to our move from Roanoke to Memphis, I felt a particular kind of anxiety that had nothing to do with packing our things or renting a moving truck or buying a house. Instead, I worried about the place itself. In the temperate mountains of Virginia, where seasons were vivid and delineated, I'd been reassured by the predictable patterns of the world, and had been able to avoid constantly worrying about the earth's rising temperatures. In fall and winter, we hiked. In summer, we paddled our canoe down tumbling river rapids. In spring, we cleared the dead brush from our garden and prepared for the first growth of the season pushing up from the thawed ground.

But in Memphis, I can't distinguish one season from another: it rains for months, it's hot for months, and that's the whole year. In the last days before we left Virginia, I relished the cool mornings shrouded in mist, and the way the day's heat dissipated by evening, and thought of Memphis' increasingly long, sweltering summers with a growing sense of dread.

Experts in a range of fields have been developing language to express the distress caused by environmental change. Philosopher Glenn Albrecht coined the terms "psychoterratic" to describe mental health related to the environment, and "solastalgia" to describe the sense of dislocation that comes with experiencing a rapidly changing environment. He described *solastalgia* as "the loss of the present," or "a form of homesickness one gets when one is still at 'home.'" In her essay "The Marsh at the End of the World," Elizabeth Rush writes, "What I used to call climate anxiety has become more like a disease. I call it endsickness. Like motion sickness or seasickness, endsickness is a physical response to living in a world that is moving in unusual ways, toward what I imagine as a kind of event horizon."

As Colin and I contemplated having a child one day, I had the sense that parenting and the climate crisis would both require wider networks of care, a shift from the individual nuclear family unit to something wider: a gift—a privilege—that I tapped into when we moved home. In 2017, in Memphis, the housing market was not quite as apocalyptic, itself, as it would be in three or five years. It took a first-time home buyer loan, mortgage insurance, all of our savings, and $5,000 from my grandmother to buy our 100-year-old bungalow.

Our first summer in the Compound, we lost power when a straight-line wind tore through the city. My brother-in-law and I were the only ones at home, and we lugged the generator from my parents' garage out into their yard. Storm clouds passed overhead as my brother-in-law and I got the generator started, plugging in extension cords to keep a refrigerator and a box fan running in each house, then stood for a moment, staring at the vibrating machine, rumbling so loud we could hardly hear each other over it.

In some unarticulated way, this too was part of my desire to move home—not only to be close to my family when trouble came, not only to raise a child surrounded by multiple generations, but to also share resources we wouldn't have been able to afford on our own. Throughout college, I'd lived with seventeen housemates in a crumbling Italianate mansion perched on the edge of our tiny Ohio town. The house had been known as the Peace and Justice House and had existed as an intentional community of students for more than thirty years before I ever lived there. In addition to a commitment to activism and a single, grimy shower, my housemates and I shared chores, meals, and, most importantly, a costume closet. For years, it seemed I was never in a car alone; anybody's trip to the grocery, or the airport, or Chipotle, became an occasion for carpooling, groups of us piled in the backseat, requesting whatever additional stops we needed on the way. In the six years that passed between graduation and our move to the Compound, I'd missed the thrum of a more communal life, of the way it felt to live within a broader community who took interest and active participation in each other's lives.

In the Compound, our three households didn't need three lawn mowers: We shared yard tools, borrowed cars when one was stuck in the shop. We watched each others' pets and mowed each others' lawns. We cooked for each other or, when one household cooked extra, left Tupperware on back porches to share. In the winter, when we lost power, we crowded around my parents' fireplace and took turns keeping soup warm on the stove. One night, standing on the back deck watching an owl fly soundlessly from one tree to the next, I looked next door and saw my parents were standing in their yard, barefoot in pajamas, watching him, too.

I spent the night of that first power outage—what would be the first of many—sleepless and hot, listening to the generator hum. I was acutely aware of how close we were to my entire family, how quickly we could get to them if we heard the sound of a tree falling, or glass breaking, or the tornado sirens wailing eerily as they had done off and on all day. The nickname for our new home—the Compound—disturbed me. It seemed militaristic, as if we lived in a fortress surrounded by unseen enemies. I comforted myself by thinking of *compound*'s other meanings: *a mixture composed of two or more separate elements*, or as a verb: *to put together, so as to form a whole.*

A few years ago, I started noticing bumper stickers on passing cars reading, "Not of This World," or simply the letters *NOTW* drawn as a single, swirling graphic, the "T" looming over the other letters like a distended cross. The phrase is a truncated reference to John 17, when Jesus says, "I have given them your word and the world has hated them, for they are not of the world any more than I am of the world." Later, he reiterates: "My kingdom is not of this world."

My parents referenced this verse often when I was growing up, but I was surprised to see its widespread use, those four letters a shorthand for something I didn't quite understand. For my parents, this verse was a reminder not to be materialistic, not to hoard possessions or participate in mindless consumerism. But I felt certain this was not the meaning people intended to signify with this abbreviation. When I asked my husband, I learned that he was taught that this verse meant that Christ's followers should always be prepared to leave this world behind for God's better world beyond. They were *not of this world*—they belonged somewhere else, and would be going there soon.

These two interpretations of this single phrase—*Not of This World*—could not be more different. One seems so dualistic—not *this* world but *that* one—while the other emphasizes how to live life here, in this world, the only world we know we have. And while it's difficult for me to imagine an unseen world beyond this one, it's impossible to imagine *longing* for another world.

I've asked my husband many times to explain how anticipating the apocalypse works in everyday life. Even if I believed in a world-ending apocalypse, I told him, I couldn't imagine being excited about it. Weren't evangelicals, even secretly, a little scared?

"The thing is," Colin said, "what is promised at the end of the world is supposed to be so much better than this world."

We talked as we drove down a tree-lined street, light streaming through the green leaves. I couldn't imagine anything better than this world. When I told him so, he sighed. He is my evangelical-whisperer.

"There will be no debt," he elaborated. "No financial stress, no mental or physical illness. All your lost loved ones will be reunited."

I thought about the way I felt, many mornings, when I woke to news of hurricanes or wildfires, families rebuilding their homes again and again or forced, finally, to flee. When I read that an elderly couple in Memphis had frozen to death during a power outage after a freak winter storm, or watched a video of kangaroos bounding across a burning hillside, or saw photos of a farmer's failed crops grown in saline soil, I felt something like a weight, dark and heavy, settling over my chest, and an anxious urge to fling it away.

Perhaps that feeling was not so different from longing for some other world, for some escape, for a life that didn't feel so uncertain and fraught.

Of course, some evangelical Christians might not fear the apocalypse because they believe they will be spared during the rapture, spirited away before the suffering begins here on earth. The idea of the rapture is relatively new, popularized by the nineteenth-century evangelist John Nelson Darby and later spread widely by the Scofield Reference Bible, which included Darby's writings on the rapture in the margins. Though a belief in the rapture might hover somewhere on the edges of conservative evangelical Christianity, it seems, in some ways, like the logical conclusion for *Not of This World* thinking, for any theology that imagines the world could end and the faithful could, somehow, go on without it.

There has long been an argument that a belief in the apocalypse explains conservative evangelicals' skepticism of climate change. If one believed that the earth was destined to be destroyed in a final, God-sent, world-ending flame, why should we work to conserve habitats, or protect endangered species, or enact global emissions standards, or make any other efforts to reverse the effects of climate change? What is the point of saving this world, when there is another, better world to come? To premillennialists, the world getting worse is a sign that Jesus is close at hand. And the idea of manmade climate change—and the urgent calls to do something about it—could both be seen as a challenge to God's omnipotence: If God is all powerful, then humans can't change the climate—and if the climate is changing, it must be part of God's plan.

In *The Gospel of Climate Skepticism,* Robin Globus Veldman, an interdisciplinary environmental studies scholar, calls this the "end times apathy hypothesis." But she counters that conservative evangelicals of varying theological or denominational backgrounds often do not agree about how to interpret climate change. Some, which she calls "hot millennialists," see climate change as a possible sign of fast-approaching end-times. Others, which she calls "cool millennialists" do not necessarily see climate change as a sign of the end-times;

instead, these Christians argue, climate change is a secular apocalypse, a distraction.

Either way, the end result is the same: Whether climate change is a sign of the end or a distraction from it, there is nothing to be done about it.

Veldman argues that conservative evangelical Christians' skepticism of climate change does not stem from a lack of understanding of the science. More education, more compelling stories, and more frightening data will not solve this problem. Instead, their skepticism of any action to curb climate change stems from a general sense of embattlement that lies at the heart of evangelical Christians' identity.

To many evangelicals, Veldman writes, climate change is simply "a hoax—a competing eschatology concocted by secularists who sought to scare people into turning to government instead of God." In the secular apocalypse of climate change, God is not in control, and no one is spared: what remains of the world as we know it will go on without all of us, rather than the faithful continuing on without the world.

Months after visiting my in-laws in Kentucky, I found myself watching recorded worship services on their church website. Several sermons about Noah and the flood drew to a close with a discussion of the end of the world. In one, the pastor began, "What's unique about the Christian faith is that Christianity is the only faith system that identifies the problem with the world as something squarely within us. We're the problem. And the solution is something wholly outside of us."

"God's gonna judge the world again," my in-laws' pastor intoned on my laptop screen, one pixelated hand in the air. "This time, not by flood but by fire."

He almost looked sorry, when he said there was nothing we could do to save ourselves.

Whenever I opened my phone, reflexively, many times a day, my eyes glided past news stories I was no longer able to read all the way through: The last female Yangtze giant softshell turtle in captivity died following artificial insemination; whales showed up on beaches with bellies full of plastic bags; a heat wave across India climbed to 122 degrees Fahrenheit; a UN report warned that a million species were on the brink of mass extinction. I felt my heart rate jump with each bit of frantic bad news, but my thumb slid past, hurrying each headline beyond my sight.

Though the intense heat and humidity in Memphis increased my anxiety about climate change, the distance I felt from the natural world, here in the city, made it harder to be sure of the ways this particular place was already changing. In some places, the future predicted by climate modeling is clearly already here: In coastal towns devastated by hurricanes and chronic flooding, some residents have petitioned local governments to help them leave rather than rebuild; across Texas, rolling blackouts left much of the state in flooded darkness; wildfires sent sky-obliterating smoke around the globe.

But here in my landlocked, Southern hometown, which has always felt less-than-hospitable, changes have not been so dramatic. It has always been too hot, too humid, for too much of the year. The weather has always been unpredictable and hazardous, especially for the most vulnerable people in our city, where more than 20 percent of people live in poverty. Rather than any dramatic changes in the weather, I felt, at first, a persistent sense that something was not quite right, that this place was changing in subtle ways, perceptible only with close attention.

Our first winter in the Compound, near-daily rains swept in currents from my sister's yard, across my parents' and into ours. Water stood in the saturated backyard for days, leaving arcing impressions in the sopping ground like the tide carving a path through sand.

In what little spring we had, we planted a small garden, but I struggled to grow plants like I could in Virginia. The green bean plants stayed strangely miniature, with beans the size of bobby pins dangling from tiny leaves. It was too hot, even, for tomatoes—the spindly green plants stood mostly empty, their overheated flowers unable to pollinate and make fruit.

On waning summer evenings, I stood on the back porch and watched a few sputtering lightning bugs spark across the darkening sky. At another time, I would have found them reassuring, their flickers of light a predictable part of an unpredictable landscape. But now, I watched them and wondered, *weren't there more, when I was a kid*?

Perhaps this was what Albrecht meant when he described *solastalgia* as the loss of the "potential for solace": even the natural world, when I managed to notice it, didn't comfort me anymore. Gradually, over time, the present had become merely a screen onto which I projected my anxieties about the future.

But the apocalyptic visions heralded by climate change are decidedly not futuristic. Another world is coming, one unlike anything we've ever seen, arriving every moment. It's not on some other planet, or in some other time. It's unfolding here, right now. Whenever a patch of Siberian tundra burns, or rain falls on a Greenland icecap, or a coastal marsh is inundated with saltwater and releases more carbon into the atmosphere, the world we've known slips further from view.

I never actually read the Book of Revelation, in all my years growing up in the church. I guess I took my dad's instruction seriously, when all the children were secreted out of the sanctuary's back door. But when I recently asked my dad about that Sunday, he told me my memory was wrong.

"I wasn't preaching about the Book of Revelation," he said. "I remember on that Sunday, I wanted the kids to leave because I planned to quote Will Campbell."

"What was the quote?"

"'We're all bastards, but God loves us anyway,'" he said.

My brain started spinning, trying to reorient. I could remember that Sunday so clearly. I remembered the ominous feeling that loomed over me as we exited the sanctuary, and I remembered wondering what was lurking in that secret, sacred text, that my father would try and hide it from me. But no, he just didn't want to say the word "bastard" in front of a bunch of kids. What was even more strange: my only memory of my father preaching from the Book of Revelation didn't actually exist.

I was thirty years old when I turned to the Bible's final pages to read the Book of Revelation for the first time. The book's author, John—who may or may not be the same author as the Gospel of John—wrote from exile in a cave in Patmos. He'd seen a vision of Christ, who instructed him: "Now write what you have seen, what is, and what is to take place after this." John recorded a vision of the physical world's destruction: the sun turned black and the moon, red as blood; "the sky vanished like a scroll rolling itself up"; even the stars fell to earth.

Many Christians now interpret the Book of Revelation—originally titled *apocalupsis* in Greek—as a prophecy for the end of the world. But in Greek, *apocalupsis* means "unveiling" or "uncovering." Similarly, though *Revelation* has become synonymous with a prophecy for the end of the world, the word's original meaning refers to a flash of new understanding, often seeming to come from outside of ourselves. Rather than a new world, revelation leads to new sight, a new way of seeing the world that's always been there.

In Revelation, when the earth as we've known it has passed away, God's kingdom to come is also conveyed in earthly language: there is a river "bright as crystal," a fruit-bearing "tree of life." Even after the supposed end of the world, there is life abundant, "healing of the nations," a world un-degraded. "Nothing accursed will be found there anymore."

It seemed there was no real end of the world to be found here—only massive and continual change, not so unlike the world we live in now. I wonder if change might be harder to imagine—maybe even harder to bear—than a definitive end.

There are plenty of scriptural interpretations that affirm that this world is God's kingdom—not some other world, or at some other time. In some translations of Luke 7:20–22, when the Pharisees ask Jesus when the Kingdom of God will come, Jesus answers, "The kingdom of God will not come with observable signs. Nor will people say, 'Look, here it is,' or 'There it is.' For you see, the kingdom of God is in your midst."

Even in Revelation, the new city to come descends from heaven to earth, and the book's author promises that "the home of God is among mortals. He will dwell with them."

In the Gospel of Thomas, an apocryphal collection of Jesus's sayings, the disciples ask Jesus many times to describe the future they anticipate. When they ask Jesus when the new world will come, Jesus responds, "What you look forward to has already come, but you do not recognize it." Later, he says, "The Kingdom of the Father is spread out upon the earth, and men do not see it." At one point, the disciples ask Jesus how "our end will be," and Jesus responds, "Have you discovered, then, the beginning, that you look for the end? For where the beginning is, there will the end be."

I've often wondered how these old stories, written in the midst of "their then" still manage to speak to this world, to "our now." I've always sympathized with these anxious disciples, asking over and over again what the future will be like, and being told only to look around them; being told, over and over again, *this.*

Removing the promise of another world, the challenge of faith shifts: rather than waiting for some unseen world to take this one's place, faith becomes about seeing this world as singular and sacred.

Lately, it has felt painful to stay awake to a world so clearly suffering; difficult to experience wonder or holiness on these patches of earth I am no longer sure I recognize, almost impossible to be present to a changing world without knowing how this story will end.

But a faith without an apocalypse—where there is no rapture, no promise of escape from this world to some other unseen, unscarred one—might be a way back to this world, not away from it. This kind of faith mirrors the uncertain world in which we live, the one that never really ends but keeps on changing.

Reading the Book of Revelation, I found myself returning to the description of the beast that "was and is not and is to come." Some pastors would say the beast is the devil, Satan himself. Some might see the beast as corrupt, worldly kingdoms that will rule until Christ returns. My father would say the beast could symbolize authoritarian governments and oppressive systems that have a way of mutating and reappearing, from age to age.

But it's the phrasing itself—"was and is not and is to come"—that intrigues me. It's an example of my favorite linguistic trick of these old texts, their braiding of past, present, and future to express in the rhythm of language itself something about the nature of God, or the world, or of God in the world.

It brings to mind the hymn in which we sang about what "wert, and art, and evermore shalt be," that playful, poetic configuring of verb tenses that somehow shifts the ground beneath my feet, bringing past, present, and future into one moment I am always currently in. Whenever we sang the doxology, which I knew by heart long before I could read, I always loved that perfect last line, that promise or plea, circling back on itself: "As it was in the beginning/ is now and ever shall be/ world without end/ amen, amen."

WELCOME TO
Kentucky
UNBRIDLED SPIRIT
Birthplace of Abraham Lincoln

THE ARK AT THE END OF THE WORLD

WHEN WE ARRIVED AT the Ark Encounter, just a few minutes after it opened for the day, the parking lot was already full. We sat in our car and watched families and youth groups wander from their minivans and church buses—many with license plates from Michigan, Minnesota, and Wisconsin still crusted in ice and salt—to purchase tickets and board buses that would shuttle them to the ark. My husband, Colin, and I had been in high spirits on the morning's hour-long drive from Louisville, listening to music and pointing out bands of deer grazing in the fields on either side of the highway. Now we couldn't force ourselves to get out of the car.

On the drive that morning I'd watched the outside world roll by, a landscape of in-betweens: Not quite hilly or flat; neither wholly southern or midwestern. A 500-foot-long replica of Noah's Ark might seem strange anywhere, but this monument to certainty felt especially out of place in this particular place, where nothing seemed quite settled. On that mid-February morning, northern Kentucky hovered between seasons—yellow grass still crisp with frost under a bright, warming sun. We'd stayed up late, the night before, on strange corners of the internet, watching vlogs: groups of atheists smugly debriefing in the parking lot after touring the ark, or Christian families with five or seven or nine children taking pilgrimages there, traveling in hulking vans across several state lines. We read reviews in which even the believers complained of the ark's too-small signage, confusing layout, and the $10 parking fee.

One reviewer noted that "it was odd to see dinosaurs on the ark." Another said, "Christians will want to spend a lot of time here." Everyone loved the buffet.

We bought tickets and boarded the bus, where the speakers blasted music reminiscent of *The Hunger Games*. The bus passed through the shadow of what I thought, at first, were guard towers, like those looming over prison grounds, until I realized they were stations in a zip line that, in warmer weather, swept visitors over the forested, gentle hills. The bus dropped us off at the gift shop and we walked the winding pathway toward the boat. This must have been the "encounter" emphasized in the attraction's name; the ark itself is hidden far from the road, so that when you see it clearly for the first time, you are arriving on foot, as if you're one of the lucky few allowed to board before disaster comes. This set-up—including the parking fee and tickets purchased in the parking lot a bus ride away—makes it impossible for people to drive by the ark to gawk or take photos for free, ensuring that you and your fellow visitors are here in good faith.

Except that we weren't. Colin, a Kentuckian who grew up attending an evangelical church in a former shopping mall—nearly broke out in hives when I asked him to visit the Ark Encounter with me. I've always been fascinated by evangelical Christianity: its certainty and urgency are so foreign to the quiet, painstakingly moderate tradition I'd been raised in. And as I've lost my footing in any particular belief system, I've wondered with increasing frequency what it would feel like to be certain about something—about anything.

The Ark Encounter is operated by Answers in Genesis, a young-earth creationist organization founded by Ken Ham in 1994. Answers in Genesis also owns the Creation Museum, forty-five miles away, in Petersburg, Kentucky. Both attractions aim to promote young-earth creationism and a literal interpretation of the Bible and, ostensibly, to make a lot of money: The $73 million Ark Encounter opened in 2016 with the help of $18 million in state tax incentives, despite Answers in Genesis requiring employees to testify to their Christian faith on their hiring paperwork.

The Ark Encounter and the Creation Museum have quickly become the largest tourist attractions in the area, and their closest competitors are vying not just for crowds but for distinct understandings of the world. This area of northern Kentucky—as well as bands of southwest Ohio and southeastern Indiana—are home to the Cincinnatian fossils, dating back more than 443.7 million years, and the map surrounding the Ark Encounter and the Creation Museum is studded by fossil parks, fossil outlet stores, geology museums, and art galleries specializing in "geo rarities."

Depending on which roadside attraction you choose, you'll be presented with opposing visions of the world and its origins: one in which the world is billions of years old and the product of constant, ongoing change; or one in which the world is more like 6,000 years old and in which all of earth's life forms were created, fully formed, in only six days. To young-earth creationists, evolution remains, at best, just an unsubstantiated, incorrect hunch. At worst, according to Henry Morris, one of the founding fathers of young-earth creationism, evolution is a "tool of Satan to destroy belief in God."

At the opening of the Creation Museum in 2007, Ken Ham referenced the 1925 Scopes trial and promised that the Creation Museum would serve as a reversal to the humiliation suffered by creationists when the defense attorney Clarence Darrow called prosecuting attorney William Jennings Bryan as an expert on the Bible and interrogated him on the witness stand. The Scopes trial "was the first time the Bible was ridiculed by the media in America," Ham said. He made a promise: "We are going to undo all of that." In the Creation Museum and the Ark Encounter, Ham aims not only to rewrite history, but to create a future in which creationism is no laughing matter.

We entered the Ark through the belly of the boat, into a dark room filled with empty wooden cages stacked from floor to ceiling. There was little signage and no clear direction in which to travel, so we wandered aimlessly, looking up at the ship's organs, dim lanterns hanging from the wooden beams overhead. Sounds of a storm at sea roared through the speakers—thunder cracking at surprising intervals, waves crashing against the side of the ship, people moaning, animals crying out, the wooden boat itself groaning under the strain of the storm. In the midst of it all, we came across an animatronic version of Noah's family, mid-prayer, fallen to their knees.

"Noah, that's my name!" exclaimed one kid, who we would come to find was one of many children named Noah running around this boat.

In the second room, the cages lining the walls were larger, and filled with unmoving replicas of each animal "kind." (Young-earth creationists use the word "kind," rather than "species," because this is the word used in Genesis, representing the original form as it was created by God.) As we trudged in a single-file line past the cages, people held their cellphones up to the wooden bars and took photos of the animals, with their plastic sheen, sitting in their dark cells.

According to the Ark Encounter, the 6,744 animals on board the ark included "up to 85 kinds of dinosaurs." To young-earth creationists, dinosaurs did not evolve over time, with different species existing in distinct eras separated by millions of years; they were all created on the same day, and most of them were either wiped out by humans after Adam and Eve were expelled from the Garden of Eden, or perished in the flood. (A graphic on the Creation Museum website shows a man and a stegosaurus treading the rising floodwaters, side-by-side, with the ark looming in the background.) Before Adam and Eve ate the forbidden fruit, dinosaurs had coexisted peacefully with humans; it was only later that dinosaurs and humans began to have trouble. In one Ark Encounter video—which a boy ran past and pronounced *boring!*—a muscled, CGI Adam cuddled a brontosaurus.

The Ark Encounter argues that the location of fossils discovered throughout the Earth's layered substrata tells us nothing about their age, or the eons that separated them; instead, these remains are located wherever the floodwaters deposited them as they swept across the Earth's surface and retreated. Some young-earth creationists believe that fossils are actually false evidence planted by God to tempt us from the Biblical truth.

The Ark Encounter was built using dimensions taken from Genesis: 300 cubits was translated to 510 feet; the exterior of the boat was constructed with a mix of cypress and pine. This is one of the strengths of the story of Noah and his ark for proponents of Biblical literalism; the story comes with the specific measurements, precise numbers of animals, and exact amounts of time, that make this kind of replica possible. But in their emphasis on recreating the ark—simply to prove it was possible to fit two of every animal "kind," as well as Noah's family, onto a single vessel—the creators of the Ark Encounter have reduced the story to its barest details, draining it of any larger, non-literal significance.

Behind us in line, a small boy

stared at a pair of Scutosauruses cowering in their dark cell. He asked his mom, in a small, worried voice, how all these animals survived the flood. His mother seemed genuinely stricken, overcome with emotion.

"How did *God* even survive?" she said, in a near-whisper.

Perhaps this kind of sensory dramatization, itself, is the point: the Ark Encounter allows us to stand in Noah's rope sandals, walk around his loud, dimly-lit boat, and try to imagine experiencing a storm of such magnitude that it gave us the "biblical proportions" by which we now describe weather events that once seemed rare and extreme. We can wander the ship's bowels, listening to the recorded waves crashing all around us, and wonder what it would be like, to feel so much fear, and to have so much faith.

On the Ark's second deck it took me a full minute, staring at a llama whose ears rotated precisely from side to side, to discern that the animal was real, and not an animatronic replica. Other than a single dark corner reserved for a strange mix of live animals—two llamas, a tortoise, and a porcupine scuffling around in fresh hay—the rest of the second deck was occupied by the same type of animal statues as those we saw below. The large cages were filled with "kinds" of animals I'd never seen before—strange-looking super-sized bears (which I would be tempted to describe as "prehistoric") towering alongside miniature hippos—but these cages took up only the center of the ship. Surrounding the cages were exhibits on subjects like the fall of man, the dangers of children's book depictions of the ark, and the origins of different ethnicities.

Not surprisingly, young-earth creationists hold some disconcerting views about race, like their contention that the women that Noah's sons married, some of them lighter-skinned, and some of them darker, would go on to determine the various ethnicities of the world. But some of their other arguments—about how evolutionary ideas have often been used for racist ends, justifying everything from eugenics movements to genocide—felt startlingly clear-eyed.

What came across most clearly in these wide-ranging exhibits is the sheer contempt that the Ark Encounter's creators hold for both the "pre-flood world," and our own, which they see as mirrors of each other. In an exhibit titled "Descent into Darkness," dioramas showed miniature, scantily-clad women dancing around bonfires, and men battling giants and dinosaurs in gladiatorial rings, surrounded by jeering crowds. Above us, a message printed in capital letters ran the length of the exhibit: "THE PRE-FLOOD WORLD WAS EXCEEDINGLY WICKED AND DESERVED TO BE JUDGED...DOES OUR SIN FILLED WORLD DESERVE ANY LESS?"

I watched as a father lifted his toddler into his arms and held him close to one of these dioramas, in which tiny and incredibly realistic people were contorted in all kinds of suffering. The child whimpered, burying his face in his father's shoulder. He looked sleepy. How weird, I thought, to bring a baby here.

"Look," the man said, rotating his body so that the little boy would again face the diorama. "Daddy wants you to see."

By the third floor, the animals had disappeared, and we wandered through a rapid-fire re-writing of natural history. The Ice Age exhibit I'd wanted to see because it dealt more directly with climate change was closed to the public for "defrosting," but other exhibits expounded on evolution, carbon dating, and the age of the earth, contrasting "the evolutionary worldview" with "the Biblical worldview." We shuffled along with tightly-packed crowds through an exhibit that asked how "evolutionists" and "creationists" can consider the same evidence and come to different conclusions: "Our conclusions are strongly influenced by our worldviews," the sign argued. "Which worldview makes better sense of the evidence?"

I'd never thought of myself as a person with a "worldview." In my father's churches, I was taught that science and religion were compatible—not competing—sources of truth, echoing evolutionary biologist Stephen J. Gould's formulation that science and religion explore "non-overlapping magisteria." This made any tensions I felt between faith and the world negotiable, a question of my ability to hold multiple perspectives in tension, rather than choosing one over the other.

When I first read about Ken Ham, Answers in Genesis's founder, I was surprised to find that he came to young-earth creationism while working as a science teacher in Australia, where he grew up. "I took students to museums and saw that all the museums were totally from an evolutionary perspective," he told a *Washington Post* reporter in 2017. Ham began researching and lecturing on creationism. "[J]ust because a majority believes in something doesn't mean it's right," he said. "People love darkness rather than light. If a majority believes something, I'm naturally suspicious because of the sin nature of man."

This suspicion of science is not limited to young-earth creationism; it's baked into the formation of the larger evangelical movement. In the early twentieth century, conservative Christians became increasingly wary of the modernism and liberalism they saw all around them: The country was becoming more diverse and more concentrated in cities; other protestant denominations were accepting evolution; even the authorship of several books of the Bible had come up for debate. But the Scopes trial of 1925, which Ham referenced at the Creation Museum's grand opening, was a particularly galvanizing moment for white evangelicals who felt increasingly alienated: "The ignominy surrounding the Scopes trial convinced evangelicals that the larger culture had turned against them," historian Randall Balmer writes in *The Making of Evangelicalism*. Evangelicals "responded by withdrawing from the culture, which they came to regard as Satan's domain, to construct an alternative universe, an evangelical subculture."

These first subcultures included Bible colleges, publishing houses, and seminaries, but soon expanded beyond the explicitly religious realm. In *The Anointed: Evangelical Truth in a Secular Age,* evangelical scholars Randall J. Stephens and Karl W. Giberson described the growing (and increasingly lucrative) "parallel cultures" of the contemporary evangelical world: in addition to Christian music, books, and movies, evangelical leaders and organizations produce "in-house versions of natural science, history, social science, and views of the end-times."

More recently, young-earth creationists have established their own parallel cultures in the form of peer-reviewed journals and research institutes seeking to prove their theories about creation and the age of Earth. There is even a Creation Wiki, virtually identical to Wikipedia, but "written from the Biblical worldview." The efficacy of these parallel cultures allows evangelicals to "reject the non-Christian world around them." In a 2010 speech, Ken Ham echoed this sense of a definitive binary, arguing that there was "no neutral position" between biblical literalism and atheism.

Wandering the Ark Encounter, I couldn't help thinking about the fact of its timing. As global temperatures and sea levels rise, the future is increasingly uncertain. Many scientists don't agree on the specific effects of climate change, and modeling is limited—can we stave off the worst effects by capping temperature rise at 1.5 degrees Celsius, or will 2 degrees be enough? Will oceans rise globally a certain number of inches, or feet? Will we lose all of Boston to rising seas, or just select streets? At the Ark Encounter, none of these questions exist: The rising temperatures we see now are either overblown, or part of the natural fluctuations the planet has seen, in cycles, over the course of its

6,000- to 10,000-year existence. Plus, God promised never to flood the Earth again, so we shouldn't worry too much about rising seas.

When I first heard of Ham and Answers in Genesis, I was struck by the insistence on "answers" in all of the organization's official materials. At the Answers Center, a sleek auditorium housed in the Ark Encounter's sprawling gift shop, Ham and a rotating cast of characters have given talks—recorded for the Answers in Genesis podcast and reprinted in *Answers* magazine—on subjects like "grace not race relations" and "the forensics of God's fingerprint design." The tagline on their website reads, "Don't Just Wonder. Get Answers." At a time when answers about the future are hard to come by, Ham is eager to give the people what they want.

Some refer to young-earth creationism as "anti-intellectual," but this doesn't really seem representative of what's going on here. The kind of Christianity on display in the Ark has its roots in the Christian apologetics movement, when, following years of cultural withdrawal, evangelicals emerged armed with a central scripture, in which the apostle Paul instructs believers to "always be prepared to make a defense" of their faith, ready with an answer to every question. Even as young-earth creationists reject the findings of science, they appropriate its logic and rationalism, as if through these tools they could create an airtight faith that can't be disproved. From the inside, young-earth creationism offers a logical-sounding answer to every question. From the inside, this world makes perfect sense.

It was surprisingly unsettling to see the familiar setting of the natural history museum reappropriated in order to undermine scientific knowledge and methods of inquiry. But it is a very specific understanding of science on display at the Ark Encounter, a version of science that is adversarial, that seeks to prove, explain, and dismiss, rather than to probe, question, and describe. And it is this posture that the creators of the Ark Encounter seek to emulate: faith as an argument, as opposition, faith as a kind of certainty—as a kind of science.

But a literal interpretation of the Bible that would see scripture as a scientific explanation for the world demands that scripture operate in a mode that simply didn't exist at the time of its writing. Forcing an origin story to retroactively act as science is far more radical than understanding scripture as metaphor or poetry, as a way of orienting oneself and one's community to larger stories of human history, the world's origins, and the sacred.

One of the aspects of science that Ham dislikes the most is the fact that science responds to change: with new discoveries, new information, scientists respond with revised hypotheses, new theories, updated questions. It's never settled, never finished. Ham has argued that since science changes with new discoveries, it can't be trusted; the Bible is the only source of infallible, unchanging truth: "Apart from the foundation of the Bible," Ham argues, "we couldn't really know anything for certain."

When I described the Ark Encounter to my friend Daniel, who was raised in more charismatic branches of the evangelical church, he told me he often wondered if young-earth creationists might be defending themselves not against science or evolution, as they claim, but against the messiness of faith itself. He thought the rigidity of their beliefs might be motivated by a desire to contain the wild, mysterious, and contradictory aspects of faith, by channeling it all into a rational, self-contained system, one that is only legible from within.

The strangest part of the Ark Encounter was a series of two short films—part one shown on the second floor, and part two shown on the third. In the first video, set in Biblical times, Noah hurries to complete his ark while a storm builds in the background. A sneering British journalist, adorned in piercings and tattoos, asks Noah half-hearted, condescending questions about his project, while the sky glows an ominous green, flashing with computer-generated lightning.

In the second video, set in the present-day, a cynical journalist played by the same actor as in the first film visits the Ark Encounter and is so moved by a video, just like the one we're watching now, that she converts to Christianity. "Every year," a man guiding her through the wonders of the Ark Encounter tells her, "fifty million people are swallowed by this black hole called death." The journalist's mouth hangs open. She's no longer ironic, detached, or surly. "You don't have to get religious," the man assured her. "You don't have to change who you are...You get to trade your judgment in for [Christ's] perfection."

I was struck by the formulaic presentation of what a life of faith was supposed to mean: give this, get that. An exchange. And though the video showed the journalist transformed, shaken to her core by the experience of visiting the Ark Encounter, her conversion is not so much from doubt to faith as it is from fear to certainty. While the video seemed to depend on the viewer sharing a similar experience, it was uninspiring to the point of meaninglessness for the uninitiated, for the outsider it purportedly hopes to reach.

The writer Meghan O'Gieblyn, a former young-earth creationist, described Ken Ham's projects as "the church's latest attempt to bewitch unbelievers with glitzy multimillion-dollar productions." I wondered whether I would be considered an unbeliever. I'd found it impossible, lately, to articulate whether I felt more religious or secular, whether I felt more strongly my faith or my doubt. As we'd approached this giant ship, its smooth wooden sides faded from four land-locked years in direct sun, I had wondered whether I might be sympathetic, or even susceptible, to anything I found inside.

As we watched the videos, I was wary of my reaction to the Ark Encounter leading me to a place of certainty, a stance not unlike the Ark Encounter itself. But I was also beginning to see that the Ark Encounter was not really for unbelievers or skeptics, not for people like me, not for people looking for a spiritual or theological home. The Ark was not a tool for conversion, so much as a tool for confirmation. And once you're in, the Ark promised, you don't have to change your life. No soul-searching or good works required. You could sit secure in the fact that you had all the answers; wait for the end, don't rock the boat.

Ken Ham claims that if people were to doubt the book of Genesis, this kernel of doubt would "eventually lead to them not believing the rest of the Bible." This concern reveals the inherent precarity of literalism, of reducing faith to a formula: If any piece is removed, the whole thing falls apart. Young-earth creationism promises you'll never have to doubt. But in the end, certainty might be a barometer, not for the strength of one's faith, but for its fragility.

If God's existence cannot be known, but must be affirmed by faith, this might be why I began to feel, wandering the Ark, that this place doth protest too much. In the Ark Encounter, there is nothing that cannot be known by simply reading the Bible. There is no Kierkegaardian leap of faith, either. The theology I encountered at the Ark Encounter had been stripped of the essence of any experience of faith that I'd ever known: a sense that some things are unknowable but still worth questioning; that a spiritual life takes shape within those questions that have no answers; that glimpses of the divine are always only glimpses—fleeting moments of revelation and surprise—that open not to concrete answers, but to a deeper sense of the unknown.

After visiting the Ark, curious about my own tradition's stance on science, I looked up the United Methodist Church's Book of Discipline and found a chapter on "The Natural World" with a lengthy section devoted to "Science and Technology": "We preclude science from making authoritative claims about theological issues and theology from making authoritative claims about scientific issues," the discipline read. "Science and theology are complementary rather than mutually incompatible. We therefore encourage dialogue between the scientific and theological communities and seek the kind of participation that will enable humanity to sustain life on earth and, by God's grace, increase the quality of our common lives together."

The religious tradition I was raised in never demanded that I choose it and forsake all else, so I never did. The certainty of a more conservative theology might be a more effective tool for retention rates; as mainline Protestant churches like my father's have hemorrhaged members, non-denominational evangelical churches have swelled in size. I never had to choose between the world of faith and the world itself, and I've wondered if my ease in the world contributed to my ultimate, ambivalent wandering from the church.

For believers who feel more tension between faith and the world, perhaps there is some comfort in leaving the secular world behind in favor of one that hews more closely to their own beliefs. In the end, this is what certainty requires: a self-imposed exile, turning away from this world, from "our common lives together," in which so little is certain after all.

Though Ham claims he chose to locate his attractions in Kentucky because of its central location, he might as well have surveyed the American political landscape and planted his flag at the epicenter of white evangelicalism. Because although Senate Majority Leader Mitch McConnell is deeply disliked in Kentucky, his own home state, his voting record adheres to the conservative evangelical line, and he has been reelected five times since 1984. In this way, Ham's decision to land in Kentucky feels calculated. Though the Ark felt strangely out of place as we drove up that morning, the more I thought about it, the more Kentucky seems like the perfect home for a site of such contradictions.

The Ark Encounter encompasses more ironies than can be named. That a monument to young-earth creationism exists alongside ancient fossil deposits encapsulates some of them. That, in 2019, this roadside attraction famous for denying humanmade climate change sued its insurance company for $1 million in property damage, following unseasonably heavy rains, gestures toward a few more. But the fact that the Ark Encounter opened the same year that Donald Trump was elected president, with the help of the white evangelical voting bloc, highlights the most essential irony of the Ark Encounter: Its mission is not religious at all, but political.

The Ark Encounter celebrates a culture in which any knowledge stemming from any source other than a single, ancient text is relative, mutable, and untrustworthy. This is conceived as being apart from the world—being *from it,* but not *of it*—and it manifests in larger trends like Christian homeschooling, the anti-vaxxer movement, and the Christian right's willingness to support a president who shares none of their purported values or beliefs but does share the sense of self-imposed cultural estrangement and political embattlement that is at the core of the white conservative American evangelical identity.

In the weeks after we toured the Ark, the country abruptly shut down as the coronavirus pandemic swept across the globe. My husband and I often joked that if we'd known the world was about to end, we would not have chosen the Ark Encounter for our last road trip. In April, just before Kentucky Governor Andy Beshear was to announce updated COVID-19 casualty totals, protesters swarmed the capitol building and demanded he reopen the state. Some protesters held signs reading, "No King but Jesus." As photographs of these kinds of protests went viral, one image, taken in my home state of Tennessee, stood out: a man holding a sign that read, "Sacrifice the Weak."

Though these protesters may not know it, their stance is a direct embodiment of a particular understanding of evolutionary science: survival of the fittest, a phrase coined by the philosopher Herbert Spencer in his book *Principles of Biology,* which predated Charles Darwin's *On the Origin of Species* by nearly a decade. While Darwin later applied the idea of the survival of the fittest to the biological process of natural selection, Spencer thought that it could illustrate much wider-reaching social principles: "The poverty of the incapable, the distress that comes upon the imprudent, the starvation of the idle… are the decrees of a large, farseeing benevolence." To Spencer, those individuals who survived, who managed not to slip through the cracks of poverty and illness, were not only physically, but morally, superior, chosen by a benevolent nature that weeds out the weak from the strong.

But there are other models, other stories, other interpretations. In 1902, the Russian anarchist and naturalist Peter Kropotkin published *Mutual Aid: A Factor of Evolution* which centered the pragmatic role of cooperation and reciprocity in human and animal groups. Kropotkin argued that competition between species had been overemphasized, and that natural selection promotes not just the strength and health of individual creatures, but cooperation and altruism across groups: "There is an immense amount of warfare and extermination going on amidst various species," Kropotkin wrote. "There is, at the same time, as much, or perhaps even more, of mutual support, mutual aid, and mutual defense…"

In Kropotkin's introduction to *Mutual Aid,* he distinguished (quite beautifully) the impulse toward mutual aid as something that moves beyond mere sentiment. "It is not love to my neighbour—whom I often do not know at all—which induces me to seize a pail of water and to rush towards his house when I see it on fire," Kropotkin wrote.

"It is a far wider, even though more vague feeling or instinct of human solidarity and sociability which moves me. So it is also with animals. It is not love, and not even sympathy (understood in its proper sense) which induces a herd of ruminants or of horses to form a ring in order to resist an attack of wolves."

Instead, Kropotkin wrote, this sense of solidarity is "an instinct that has been slowly developed among animals and men in the course of an extremely long evolution." Reading this, I wonder if the kind of love that Christ urged his followers toward is not unlike Kropotkin's mutual aid; a deeply ingrained sense of solidarity that we can tune ourselves back into at will, with practice, not just because our faith compels us toward it, but because it has evolved within and alongside us for millennia.

Of course, survival of the fittest embedded itself much more firmly and widely in the American cultural understanding of evolution than mutual aid, underscoring such myths as the rugged individual or the self-made man pulling himself up by his bootstraps, which continued to proliferate at these protests where homemade signs conflated Christ with empire.

Reading coverage of these protests, I sensed the way a theology focused on individual salvation surfaces in these politics which prioritize the freedom of the individual over the health—and survival—of the collective. It all seemed like a siren blaring, a warning, about the dangers of mistaking a set of social, political, and consumerist allegiances for a theology proclaiming absolute truth, and claiming to be separate from the world while remaining irrevocably tangled with the worldly forces embodied by capitalism and right-wing politics.

In November of 2021, Answers in Genesis announced plans to build a replica of the Tower of Babel on the same property as its Ark Encounter. The story of the Tower of Babel appears in Genesis, shortly after the Great Flood, when "the whole world had one language and a common speech." Noah's descendants decided to build a city with a tower that reached as high as the heavens. Genesis tells us that they wanted to make a name for themselves, and God was not impressed. God disrupted their work by confusing their language, making them incomprehensible to each other. Unable to communicate, they "scattered over the face of the earth."

Growing up in the church, this story was often recounted as a warning about hubris, or an explanation for how people ended up living all over the world, speaking so many different languages. But one thing was always very clear: God thought building the Tower of Babel was a no-good, wrong, very bad idea. While the Tower of Babel might, like the ark, have the benefit of being a physical object that can be recreated, it had an entirely different vibe. God told Noah to build the ark, the story goes. It seemed bonkers to recreate a structure God didn't want to exist in the first place.

I assumed that this story, like every other Bible story, must mean something very different to young-earth creationists. But even the Answers in Genesis website wrestled, unconvincingly, with the weirdness of this choice. "Of course, building the ark made sense since it serves as a constant reminder of both God's mercy and judgment. But why would anyone, let alone a Bible-believing ministry, want to construct a reminder of man's rebellion?"

Ken Ham himself published an article explaining his reasoning for the new attraction (which he was apparently inspired to do while watching Glenn Beck on TV), and his interpretation sounded much the same as what I'd heard growing up. "The Bible makes it clear: people rebelled against God as they built this Tower," Ham wrote. "They had disobeyed God's directive. God judged them by causing them to speak different languages."

But Ham went on to describe how the story of the Tower of Babel illustrates why there are "different people groups (not races)."

To Ham, the Tower of Babel proves that there is no such thing as race; that we are really all one people. Elsewhere on the Answers in Genesis website, they claim that the Babel attraction will "boldly confront racist and ethnocentric philosophies and practices. Most importantly, we will proclaim the only solution to racism and every other sin that besets mankind: the gospel of Jesus Christ."

It's true that race, itself, is a construct created and amended over the course of centuries to enforce hierarchies and uphold white supremacy. But it is a kind of violence to insist that peoples identities do not exist, that a person's ethnicity is not a deeply meaningful and nuanced aspect of their life but a scientific error that can be corrected with the right theology. To insist that we are all in fact "one people" is a kind of whitewashing that deliberately erases the lived experience—and lineages—of people of color.

It's clear that an organization like Answers in Genesis—and the larger body of white American conservative evangelicals—stand to benefit from their followers refusing, on a "biblical" principle, to engage in any reckoning with racism and oppression. That this new "attraction" was announced as white evangelical Christianity faces intensifying scrutiny for its relationship to white supremacy and conservative political ideologies is no coincidence: If Christianity is the solution to racism, as Answers in Genesis claims, and not inextricably part of the problem, then it is absolved of its own sins without ever having to acknowledge them, let alone repent for them.

In *This Here Flesh: Spirituality, Liberation, and the Stories that Make Us,* Cole Arthur Riley writes about the implications of humans being made, as the book of Genesis claims, in the image of God. Riley, a Black woman, admits that her own default image of God is that of a white man. "Whiteness is a force. It moves in religion in the same manner it moves in any sphere of life," Riley writes. "Some theologies say it is not an individual but a collective people who bear the image of God. I quite like this, because it means we need a diversity of people to reflect God more fully." But, Riley writes, undoing this image of God's whiteness requires more than creating new images of God: "We have to persist in observing and naming all the ways this force has obscured the face and character of God."

While I tried—and failed—to understand Answers in Genesis's decision to build a replica of the Tower of Babel, I began to suspect that this story of what had once been a tight-knit community, sharing language and place in common, and that is doomed to fragmentation and alienation, might actually be a perfect story for our polarized and polarizing time. But this interpretation, that our scattering and mutual incomprehension is a punishment for our failure to follow God's directions, is not the only one. There are, as always, other ways to read this story.

The womanist theologian Wil Gafney writes, "The Babel story is a topsy-turvy story. People reach out to heaven and are pushed away. People working together harmoniously are separated and confused. God doesn't need towers or temples to reach God's people so God directs their creative energy elsewhere. God creates diversity out of uniformity. What looks like chaos and confusion is community building. The babble of Babel is not non-sense. People found themselves able to understand some of the people around them, those people became their people and each group grew into a distinct people with their own language and culture, enriching the beauty of God's creation. God scattered them across the earth that the world might be filled with diversity."

Perhaps the Babylonians were not punished for their hubris, but for their desire to consolidate and centralize power in order to create a monolithic society. Perhaps their scattering was not really a punishment, after all, but a course correction.

Either way, I'm not sure Bible stories are best read in isolation from each other. There are larger arcs, echoes, and resonances that span the entirety of the Bible, linking narratives and sometimes undoing them. Reading these stories in isolation—separating them from each other and building monuments to them—limits the multitude of meanings that are possible when we read more holistically. Perhaps the fragmentation of the story of the Tower of Babel finds some reconciliation in Luke, when Jesus says that people "will come from east and west and north and south, and will take their places at the feast in the kingdom of God." Or in Revelation, when the author prophesied that he saw "a great multitude that no one could number," gathering before God's throne, "from every nation, from all tribes and peoples and languages."

Threads of the Babel story certainly resurface later in the story of Pentecost, when the Holy Spirit allowed the disciples to speak and understand unknown languages. All those gathered are able to understand the disciples in their own native tongues. "The lessons of Babel and Pentecost are much the same," Gafney writes. "The aftermath of both stories is a changed people transforming the world." If there is scattering and incomprehension, it doesn't stay that way.

A highlight, for many visitors to the Ark, is a replica of the giant door that would have been installed on the Ark, big enough for any dinosaur or large animal "kind" to walk through. When I read online reviews of the Ark Encounter, I saw photo after photo of kids and moms and grandpas standing in front of this door, smiling into the camera's flash.

From the photos I saw online, the significance of the door was not immediately apparent to me, and when we came upon the door at the Ark Encounter, I watched as families stopped to pose for photos in front of it. From one side, it seemed like the door could represent an invitation: swinging open, ushering you inside, safe and sound from the dangers of the world. But from the other side, the door closes in your face; you are left outside to fend for yourself.

For the people around us, perhaps the meaning of this old story begins the moment the ark's doors are sealed, and those inside know they will be safe, while everyone outside those doors is damned to drown. I have wondered how much spiritual sustenance can be provided by simply feeling that one has all the right answers. But if there is a theological meaning that the Ark Encounter offers to its visitors, this is what it boils down to: You are right, and everyone outside these doors is wrong.

Before I shared any photos of the Ark Encounter on social media, I clicked the location tag on Instagram to see what other people had posted about this place: family selfies, breathless captions about how inspiring the place was. In my Instagram stories, I shared a blurry photo of two dinosaurs in a darkened cage, and quoted a one-star review that I'd read on TripAdvisor the night before: "I don't think God would like this place."

My husband was, as usual, a little more direct. He shared a selfie taken outside the boat, his smiling face squinting into the sun. He tagged the Ark Encounter's account and wrote, "This place and all it represents is a scourge upon humanity."

The likes, from all of our like-minded friends, poured in.

CRYING IN CHURCH

I SPENT MY FATHER'S last year as a minister crying in the second row. It could happen at any time, the crying, and I was useless to stop it. I cried a couple tidy tears that disappeared as they slid down my cheeks, and I sobbed, doubled over into my lap. I choked back tears while hurrying out of the sanctuary, and I cried in my seat, wiping my face with my sleeve, too overwhelmed to leave. It could happen just before worship began, when the chatter of parishioners visiting in the aisles was broken by the sound of a bell ringing in warm, even tones, from somewhere behind us, and the voices fell silent as people scurried to their seats. Or it could happen during the chorus of a hymn I had not heard for years, but found myself humming even now, in my kitchen, up to my elbows in soapy water, the song rising nameless and half-remembered in my throat.

Sometimes it had nothing to do with the service unfolding around me, or the sanctuary I sat in, at all. It could be the ghost of some other church, any of the six my father pastored during my lifetime, or some other Sunday morning. Some memory would rise up, a glimmer I couldn't describe with any particular detail, only in flashes: I'd see myself at five years old, maneuvering around the other kids during Children's Time, vying for the seat closest to my father; or at thirteen, sneaking a peek during prayer, peering over all the bowed heads, trying to see whether my father had his eyes open too. I'd watch the light moving across the stained-glass windows and sense, in a cumulative rush, all the years we'd spent like this, my father in the pulpit and me in the pews, hurtling through time and arriving here, at what would be my father's last church.

As a child, growing up in a series of church-owned parsonages, I never lived more than a parking lot away from church. There was no separation from the church and our home, from faith and daily life, and we still define each era in our lives by the churches my father served. At Embury, my mom skipped church to clean the parsonage the day she went into labor with me. In home videos taken at St. Timothy, I was a naked toddler stomping around a kiddie pool while behind me, just beyond the chain-link fence surrounding our yard, church members waved at the camera as they arrived for Wednesday night dinner. In our parsonage at Good Shepherd, I could see the church sanctuary from every room in our small brick ranch-style house; I learned to ride my bike by pedaling back and forth between the church and our home.

At St. Timothy, during lunch in the fellowship hall, I'd sneak off to a darkened classroom to play with a blue ceramic nativity set I found in a storage closet, behind rows of white pressed choir robes and trash bags full of Christmas lights. I'd hold the woman in one hand, the man in the other, their bodies warming inside my fists. At Good Shepherd, barefoot on the side of the road, I picked blackberries and hummed hymns, whispered prayers to my purpling fingers.

The world was drenched, then, with a presence everyone around me called God; I walked with one hand aloft at my side for him to hold.

Upon ordination, a United Methodist pastor takes a vow of itinerancy; we never stayed anywhere longer than three or four years before moving into another drab, carpeted parsonage filled with mismatched furniture. My mother, who had not bet on the life of an itinerant preacher's wife, moved her family heirlooms—antique hutches, wool rugs, her mother's dining room table and chairs—from one parsonage to the next. Itinerancy intends to keep a congregation from getting too attached to any particular pastor, but it had the opposite effect on me: as we rotated through churches, as my father was the only constant, church and faith itself seemed to be increasingly defined by his presence in the pulpit.

Whenever we moved, one group of white-haired old ladies was replaced by another, all singing the same songs, all lining up to shake my father's hand in the doorway after church. They were always the same, but I was new every couple of years in school, or every few years at church. Once I finally learned everyone's names we'd move again, and find ourselves shuffled into a new, but eerily familiar, version of our lives.

Around the time I entered middle school, some churches started selling their parsonages and providing their pastors with a housing allowance, instead. We lived at increasing distances from the churches my father served. I could no longer see the church from my bedroom windows; church was not a place I could wander into whenever I wanted. God started to feel separate from my life, my home, and my body, in a way I hadn't imagined was possible. As our Sunday mornings shifted—as our commute changed from a walk across the parking lot to a drive across town—I felt a distance growing between me and God, some connection going fuzzy, like a line gone slack.

It seemed appropriate that my father's final church, simply called Faith, was a forty-five-minute drive from home, at a time when I found myself farthest removed from my childhood faith. Where church was once an extension of my home, now we traveled far beyond the city each Sunday morning. Where the fact of God's presence was once obvious to me, I now felt most aware of God as a nagging, inner yearning for something I couldn't find or name.

In the years since I left home and church, a specific image of Christianity had risen to the top of American consciousness. When I say I am a preacher's kid, I find I must quickly clarify my childhood by defining what it was not: There was no fire and brimstone, no electric guitars or sound systems or colored light filters. There were no dunk-tank baptisms, no confessions, no altar calls or testimonies.

My father was part of a group of United Methodist pastors who graduated from seminary in the early 1980s and went to work serving congregations around West Tennessee and Kentucky. His friends met in seminary or at Plowshares, an antiwar spiritual retreat center housed in an old farmhouse where some of them lived. And though I think of these preachers as my dad's friends, Plowshares is where my mom first got introduced to this group, months before she met my dad, a detail that always surprises me.

"You need to write more about your mother," Dad tells me, "in case you turn out to be a serial killer or something. People should know she's responsible for you, too."

My parents first met in 1983. Mom was single with a six-year-old daughter, Courtney. Her first husband had abandoned her a few years earlier for another woman. When my parents met, my mom was still grieving the death of her father, who had died unexpectedly, while mowing the lawn six months earlier. Mom was working selling hardware to businesses. She sang in her church's choir, and took care of her mother, who was sick with breast cancer. Dad's church, also in Milan, my mom's hometown, was planning to host a revival. Church ladies, eyeing the young preacher and the pretty single mom in the choir, did their matchmaking work, and my parents spoke briefly on the phone before meeting in person at the revival.

Mom was interested, until she saw him—black mustache, huge glasses, pea green polyester suit. (Years later, when the suit burned in a house fire, she'd joke it was the Lord's work.) As they got to know each other, she attended one of my father's Bible study groups. She'd never heard someone spend such time investigating a text, turning it over for new meanings and perspectives. She was hooked.

My mother's parents were initially skeptical about Plowshares. A month before he died, my grandfather made a point to drive by Plowshares and scope it out before mom visited for the first time. But years later, after her own mother died, my mother found she'd kept newspaper clippings about the friends my mom had made there. Greg was sued by the federal government for refusing to pay the portion of his income taxes that he calculated would be used for U.S. military spending. Randy, preaching to a congregation in which most members were employed by the local munitions factory, implored his congregants to reconsider their work producing weapons for war. Billy officiated a same-sex wedding and was subjected to a denominational hearing. They promptly removed any traces of the American flag or blue-eyed Jesus from the sanctuary. This was the common strain I noticed in my dad and all his preacher friends: a willingness, if not a desire, to challenge their congregants even as they nurtured them. And for a while, people attending churches seemed open to being pushed out of their comfort zones. But over time, that changed.

At any of the churches my father served, he always found "accomplices," people who would stick up for him, who sometimes followed him from one church to the next. But there was also, always, someone like the man who came up after my dad preached about the Good Samaritan and told him he was just "trying to get Obama reelected." When I was in college, and my father spent a year without a church, I helped him pack up his church office and move his books into a musty storage unit. At the next church, he heard parishioners whispering about him in the church foyer over donuts and watery coffee: *He's a socialist*, they said. *He doesn't read the Bible. He doesn't even believe in Jesus.* One parishioner commented obsessively on Facebook, letting my father know he would be "the only thing left standing in the rubble of the church he had destroyed."

By the time my father decided to retire, religion itself seemed to have become just another cultural signifier, but my father and his congregations didn't agree about what, exactly, their shared faith signified. For my father, faith was about inner and outer transformation, about resisting empire and oppression, and about prophetic imagination and building healthy communities. But in the church parking lot, there was a proliferation of Trump and NRA bumper stickers. The pull of evangelical megachurch culture was strong. When parishioners asked my father to wear blue jeans, claiming that even a tie was too formal, my father instead preached in his floor-length black robe and stole. My father and his cohort of preacher friends were ornery, Wendell Berry's kind of contrary: "Going against men" and hearing "a deep harmony/ thrumming in the mixture."

When I was a kid, my dad took me to school and picked me up every day. Sometimes, on our way home from school, he'd buy us chocolate Frostys from Wendy's and we'd drive home listening to Rush Limbaugh so that, as my dad said, we would know what the enemy was saying. But conservative Christianity seemed, to me, a quirky and unlikely phenomenon. By the time I arrived in college in a small town in Ohio, I had the impression that Christianity led a person to progressive politics. My college writing professor was the first person to tell me that my experience in the church, in the South, was the exception, and not the rule.

As I've grown accustomed to describing all church wasn't, it's become harder to say what it was. What did it add up to—the creaking sanctuary floors, the carpets stained with grape juice, the altars studded with dripped candle wax? All those hours we spent here, where did they lead?

In theory, the forms provided by organized religion—while inherently, and necessarily flawed—could be fruitful: the constraints of an organized structure could create space for resistance; one could envision and refine one's own sense of the divine by running up against what it was not. But in practice, the business of church rarely felt like a container against which my soul could hone itself. It was mostly tedious and frustrating, and often felt utterly disconnected from the original impulse that led any of us here in the first place.

I always imagined that the time would come for me to decide what I believed—how I felt about faith and the church and the religion I'd been steeped in—and I assumed that time would arrive with some kind of force, from somewhere outside myself. While my dad was a pastor, I'd dammed up my unresolved feelings about it all, assuming that as long as my father was somewhere climbing into a pulpit each Sunday morning, I could step back into the stream uninterrupted.

But when he stopped—when he gathered up his papers and his worn Bible and exited the sanctuary for good—when the only access point that I'd known was taken away—where would that leave me?

When I decided to attend my father's church for his last year, I hadn't gone to church regularly since before I turned eighteen. Now, twenty-eight years old, living next door to my parents, I felt I'd entered some strange time machine. Here I was again, climbing into the car with my mom on Sunday morning for a long drive to church. After more than a decade away, it was strange to enter each weekend remembering that my Sunday was already spoken for, that Sundays weren't mine anymore. No brunch with friends, no walks in the park, no lazy Sunday mornings reading in pajamas. Church bulletins piled up, falling out of my bags, my books, my jacket pockets, with notes and grocery lists scrawled between the hymns and prayer requests.

None of my friends go to church, and there was no one my age in my father's congregation. Much has been made of "the rise of the nones," the growing number of Americans, especially those in my age bracket, who, in response to surveys asking for their religious affiliation, increasingly answer *None*. This is the box my friends would check, and the box I always assumed I would check, too, if I were ever handed a survey.

And yet, when my father decided to retire, earlier than I expected, I felt an urgent need to be there, in his church, every Sunday, to encounter head on, what I'd always preferred to skirt the edges of: what it meant or means to have grown up in these spaces, these churches perched on lonely highways, or tucked into nondescript neighborhoods, where I often felt like a stranger, even though everyone knew my name.

When my parents left town for a week, I snuck into their garage where my father had begun storing boxes of his handwritten sermons as he gradually moved out of his church office. He kept his sermons in black binders, organized and neat, each binder labeled with the month and year, each sermon attached to its corresponding bulletin with paperclips now rusted and brittle.

As I flipped through the sermons, as one year rolled into the next, seasons of Lent and Advent and Epiphany receded and returned, the scriptures repeating according to the lectionary: Pentecost's flames, Jacob's ladder, the prodigal son—my dad's favorite text. Some of his stories repeat, too. He often returned to his first job, as a church janitor. "I had so many doubts," he'd say, "about the church, about all of it."

But as the scriptures and stories repeated, whenever my sister or I appear on the page, we are constantly growing, changing, discovering and being discovered. In one sermon he's watching me walk up a flight of stairs for the first time; in another, I'm a surly teenager. I never minded when he used me in a sermon. That's what he always called it, on the rare occasion he chose to warn me. "Hey, I'm using you in my sermon today," he'd say, often just as I walked into church.

Then I'd wait, anxious to see how I'd show up, in what version of myself, in what ways he saw me. I think I knew I'd get him back one day. I think I knew there was something similar in the appraising way we saw each other, in the ways we would use each other.

I wonder how it changed me, to know my father had his eye on me, to know some vision of me might show up in a sermon on Sunday. I wonder how it changed him, to look down at the pews and see me there, notebook open on my lap, waiting for him to say what I've been thinking all along.

As my father neared retirement, he started naming each "last time" he did anything: watching contractors pull into the driveway of his house, dad would say, *this is the last time I put a roof on this house*; traveling with my mom to see Paul McCartney in concert, he called to say *I figure this is the last time I'll see him play live.* When he and I traveled to Wyoming for a week-long fly-fishing class, he said *I guess this might be my last trip out west.*

The first time we traveled out west, when I was eight or nine years old, I picked fistfuls of wildflowers and my father helped me press them between the pages of his heavy, leather-bound Bible. For years after that trip, I'd be sitting in church, watching my father in the pulpit as he turned his Bible's pages, and so often I'd see him pause to remove a perfectly preserved wildflower and set it carefully aside. It seemed, then, that there was no end to them.

Growing up, my father sealed himself off in a room to write his weekly sermon. The house would go quiet, a fan humming at his feet vibrating through the hardwood floors. I'd listen through the walls to hear him whispering to himself as he wrote. Sermons, to him, were to be heard, not read, and he revised by ear—I'd hear him practicing the phrasing, trying out emphasis on one part of a sentence and then another, finding places to pause in silence.

On a gray, winter morning, I was reading at my desk when I saw the dining room light come on at my parents' house next door. I watched my father, carrying books and a notebook and a mug of hot tea, settle into the dining room table to write his last Christmas Eve sermon, a new "last time" to add to the list. A few minutes later, I felt my phone buzz. In the photo he'd texted me, a stiff purple wildflower emerged from his Bible's center spine.

Sometimes a given worship service felt so familiar—even after all the changes, even after ten years away—that it was hard for me to see it. I arrived half-glazed over, moving by muscle memory through a world of familiarity and repetition. I'd come in the side door, squeeze past the men in short-sleeved collared shirts standing around the coffee, and find my seat beside my mom on the second row, almost without thinking. Other times, I was struck by the sheer strangeness of it: checking the bulletin every few minutes to figure out where we were in the order of things, what we would do next.

One night, dad and I were running errands when a woman in his congregation who was dying of cancer asked him to visit her at home. She'd been sleeping all day, waking up around five or six in the evening and staying up, anxious and alone, all night. We stopped by the church and went to his office, where he handed me a small wooden box and asked me to help clean it while he got ready. I took the box to the kitchen and opened it to find it was a communion to-go kit, its insides encased in red velveteen. The box held a small rubber bottle, stained light purple from years of grape juice, and two small containers that could each hold a hunk of bread. I scrubbed each container and wiped them dry, feeling the shock of some small, new thing I hadn't known existed, this carry-on case ensuring God made it wherever God needed to go.

One Sunday I cried before the service even began. For as long as I could remember, someone had played a handbell in the hallway to let us know it's time to quiet down and get ready for worship. The single note would ring out—one, two, three times—until everyone found their seats and got quiet. That morning, I came late into church and found my father standing in the hallway, holding the handbell, waiting for the right moment to ring it. I could not believe it had been him, all these years, ringing the bell.

Whenever I managed not to be incapacitated by tears, I took notes during worship, jotting down things I didn't want to forget. Usually something small: the Yorkie someone inexplicably brought with them, who shrieked with surprise at the opening of every hymn; the way one elderly lady, who thought she was whispering, shouted at full volume into her husband's wrinkled ear; or the tiny old woman who told my father that his beard made him look "extinguished." But sometimes I'd take note of something I'd never really noticed before, like the way my father washed his hands with a squirt of hand sanitizer before breaking the loaf of communion bread, holding it up in the air above his head, or the way he changed up the last lines of his usual benediction, never saying exactly the same words twice.

I cried at a baby shower thrown for the church choir director, a single woman whose application to open her home to children in foster care had recently been accepted. The icing on the sheet cake read, "Who Will it *Bee*?" in blue cursive, with a cartoon bumble bee flying through the background. I cried at Christmas, when a woman in an elf costume and greasy, dyed green hair sang the most beautiful rendition of "O Holy Night" I'd ever heard, over a too-loud recording of squealing violins.

The year I spent in church, I wasn't crying in other places. I didn't find myself moved to tears in the grocery store or at home or at work. I never even arrived at church feeling emotional. I was surprised by my tears every time, unsure whether I was crying because of how far I felt from faith, or how close, how utterly within reach. It was my own self I ran up against—not the absence of God but the absence of my own will or conviction or humility—some word I didn't know how to name, whatever it would take to claim the God I'd spent long years longing for.

Though my years of ambivalence and doubt once seemed benign enough to live with, to even ignore, I found that my lack of faith—or my inability to articulate what lingering faith I might still feel—accompanied me on each Sunday's long drive, an open wound, raw and stinging.

Halfway through the year, I began to feel an anxious desire to articulate some statement of faith, even though I know these articulations—the creeds, the memorized prayers, the affirmations recited in unison—are exactly the moments when, in church, I sense some part of myself slipping away.

My father closed every sermon with his usual invitation, asking his church to pray with him: "As always," he'd say, "you're invited to join me kneeling in prayer." One Sunday, as he turned to the altar rail and lowered himself to his knees, I felt a sudden, remorseful pang wash over me: I'd heard him share this invitation to pray with him at the altar every Sunday, but I'd never heard it as an invitation extended to me. I'd never considered joining him there in prayer. And few people ever joined him there; he almost always prayed alone.

As I watched my father—his back turned to us, his head bowed as he spoke—it was hard to imagine leaving my seat, moving down the aisle, kneeling beside him. My hands began to sweat just thinking about it; I had a feeling that I'd trip over my own feet. Even the idea of it seemed corny as hell, a scene from a TV show that I didn't want to watch. But still I wondered what it said about me, that I'd never heard his invitation as one that I, myself, could accept.

What I wanted church to do was to remind me of the moments I felt connected to something other or beyond the world in which I spent my days. I wanted church to put me there, to serve as a kind of WD-40 keeping my inner hinges open and receptive to those moments so that I wouldn't miss them when they appeared. More often, church was a reminder of how far I was from this kind of vision, how ludicrous our attempts were at doing whatever it is we were trying to do here, week after week.

I have seen a ponytailed man tied to a cross, stigmata drawn on his palms with lipstick. I have seen a baby cow, rented for an Easter petting zoo, running at full tilt through the church lawn, leaving a trail of smashed Easter eggs in her wake. Some Sundays, when the piano player bungles the notes, or the soloist misses her cue, or the acolyte nearly sets his polyester robe on fire, or the wrong lyrics appear projected on the screen and we all fall silent mid-song, it seemed we just barely, by sheer force of will, made it through worship at all. As the service drew to a close, I expected everyone in the room to let out a relieved sigh, blinking in amazement: we made it, somehow, before God sent some new plague our way; best to leave before he changed his mind.

But sometimes, in our commitment to see a clumsy moment through, it swelled, and our mistakes themselves became big enough to hold us all in a kind of suspension. Those moments when everything seemed on the verge of collapse—when something went wrong, and instead of deflating, we all held on—were the moments that revealed the expansiveness I'd been looking for all along, held not in anything like perfection, but in the human error illuminating how far we are from it.

Though my dad was the one who shuttled me to and from school, picking me up for soccer or gymnastics, ushering me through the week, on Sundays, he left the house early for church, spending a few last hours going over his sermon before worship. When we still lived in parsonages, my mother, my sister, Courtney, and I walked to church together every Sunday. Very often my father would call before we left the house and ask us to bring something he'd forgotten—a prop for Children's Time, or a dish for that night's potluck dinner, or his green leather Bible with the pages trimmed in gold. Imagining it now, we seemed a strange pilgrimage, the three of us lugging these forgotten things—a quilt, a fishing net, a chalice, a casserole—up the hill or across the parking lot separating our house from the church, feeble offerings growing heavy in our arms.

Once we moved out of church parsonages, around the same time my sister moved into her first apartment, my mom started driving me to church, and I relished the hour she spent as my trapped, captive audience. At home, she was always moving, always up to something, but on Sunday drives I could ask her questions, tell her stories, listen to her favorite cooking shows on the radio. In so many ways dad *was* church, growing up, but mom was the one who got me there. It was on one of these drives that my mother told me that she gauged big life decisions by whether they made her feel closer to God or farther away. As much as any of my dad's sermons, that glimpse of my mom's internal barometer stuck with me. I liked that it was simple, and spatial, and that it relied not on theologies or hermeneutics but on trusting her own instincts.

One Saturday night in my dad's final weeks as a pastor, he texted me just as I headed to the grocery store. He'd forgotten about communion the next morning, and wondered if I could help him out. At Kroger, I bought a loaf of bread and a gallon of grape juice, and then I drove home and walked across the yard to my parents' house, grocery bags rustling at my side.

Pilgrimage is, by definition, a temporary state, equal parts venturing-into-the-world and returning. Maybe the journey home—to this patch of ground, this tenuous, inherited faith, this too-small church that would be our last—was another kind of pilgrimage. Waiting for my father to answer the door, holding a grocery bag of grape juice and bread, I felt as expectant as any devotee, my feet poised there on the threshold, the cusp of something.

The next morning, my mom had a headache and skipped church. I rode, instead, with dad. In the middle of his sermon, he looked up from his notes and said something that sounded like a thesis statement for his half-century in the pulpit: "I worry we see the Bible as a book full of answers," my father said. "I don't think it's a book that offers answers. I think it's a book that can lead us to the best questions."

That morning I noticed a line from the communion liturgy for the first time: "We proclaim the mystery of faith," my father would say, before we all responded in unison: "Christ has died, Christ is Risen, Christ will come again." I don't know why I'd never noticed the distinction implicit in his prompt. Yes, the congregation would recite the text marked in bold, but first we proclaimed the mystery. Any professed beliefs that followed were contingent, it seemed, dependent, first, on this mystery. Not on any hard-and-fast rules or black-and-white literalism or absolute truths.

After worship ended, after my father shook everyone's hand in the doorway, hung his robe in his office, turned down the thermostat, and locked up the church, he drove me home. On the way, between strip malls and parking lots, I caught sight of a rolling pasture I'd never noticed before, a hillside of horses shaking their manes in the sun: pockets of the world turned inside out, glimpsed almost by mistake.

On my father's last Sunday, a miracle: I did not cry. It was the first Sunday of Vacation Bible School, so when I arrived, feeling maudlin and dreary, I found a church transformed into a jungle-themed summer camp. The hallways had been covered in sheets of brightly-colored butcher paper, and paper monkeys hung down from the ceiling every few feet.

Dad preached his last sermon standing next to an eight-foot-tall elephant made of cardboard and wrapped in duct tape. The pianist, sitting behind the elephant's large chest, couldn't tell when to begin playing a song, so she was constantly crawling out from behind the elephant, and then, when it was time, slowly crawling back behind it, through an attenuated silence while we all waited until we heard her playing the opening notes.

Before communion, standing next to the giant duct tape elephant and behind a cardboard cutout of a meerkat, my father reminded his congregation that this ritual had no prerequisites: "You don't have to be perfect," he said. "You don't even have to be faithful. You just have to come trusting that God's going to use what we do here for our own good."

I tried to record all the details of this moment in my mind as it happened: his black robe and stole, covered in brightly colored felt shapes cut out by children some decades ago at another church, some other place. His hair, grayer than it once was, and his eyes warm and tired. He instructed us to come forward holding our hands cupped in front of us; the communion bread would be placed in our hands as a reminder that we can't take sustenance from God—it can only be given. This seems to describe something about the way faith arrives, if it ever does—as something that cannot be achieved, only received.

There is no earning this, he seemed to say. But you can keep your hands open.

TV APOCALYPSE

PERHAPS UNWISELY, MY HUSBAND and I begin watching *Doomsday Preppers* as the pandemic begins, when restaurants and businesses have closed and unemployment numbers have begun their steady climb into the tens of millions, but before the case numbers and death counts begin to soar. I'm three months pregnant, and to leave the house means wearing a mask, carrying bottles of hand sanitizer and packages of disinfectant wipes we use to shield our hands whenever we have to touch a door knob or a shopping cart. My mother comes home from a rare trip to the grocery store and describes uniformed guards stationed alongside the paper towels.

As spring turns to summer, the internet helpfully predicts "murder hornets," and hordes of cicadas louder than ever before. The Arctic Circle is on fire, and the nightly news warns of a Saharan dust cloud passing over the southeast, bringing with it asthma attacks and painfully beautiful sunsets. While the world outside my body seems on the verge of collapse, the world inside my body has charted its own course, unconcerned, making itself new.

Each prepper featured on the show is preparing for a specific end-times scenario, which they describe at the opening of the segment: "I'm preparing for total economic collapse," one man says while rappelling down the sides of the decommissioned ballistic missile silo he purchased in Kansas. "I'm preparing for the power grid to fail," they say, or for an asteroid to hit earth, or for a massive tsunami, a catastrophic earthquake. They show off hidden store rooms, get into aquaponics, build sniper towers, make plans to escape to Costa Rica.

After watching it for the first time, I go to bed anxious and uneasy. I pull out a book and read the same sentence over and over while my mind roams scenes from the TV show: the basement shelves lined with gleaming jars of preserved food, the bunkers patrolled by armed vigilantes. There were several times I'd find myself disturbed by some aspect of the show, only to see Colin, out of the corner of my eye, nodding in admiration of someone's welding skills, or their five-gallon barrels full of various kinds of seeds or grain. Lying next to me in bed, his face is peaceful and still, staring up at the ceiling.

"You prepping?" I ask him. He nods.

If my husband has retained any particular aspect of his upbringing in western Kentucky, bunker and all, it is not quite prepping, with its paranoid doomsday implications, but preparedness more generally. He has always bought things in sets of three or four that I would've bought alone. "Two is one and one is none," he'd remind me at the grocery store, adding an extra onion or jar of pasta sauce to the cart. But something—the pandemic, or my pregnancy, or the late-night episodes of *Doomsday Preppers*—kicks Colin's latent prepping tendencies into high gear.

He orders bandages, gauze, and medicine in bulk on Amazon and makes first aid kits for the bathroom, the car, the kitchen, the shed. A pared-down version of his father's basement bunker appears in our house, as Colin fills our boiler room, keeping it stocked with canned vegetables and jugs of water. He buys an emergency shovel, with a razor-sharp edge, and seems puzzled when I ask why we might need it. He keeps our chest freezer packed to the brim with chicken thighs, salmon fillets, and his father's venison. When my weeks of morning sickness finally pass, I crave fresh fruit and find shiny plastic cartons of strawberries stacked high in the fridge, or a bowl of apples, shining in the sunlight, on the dining room table.

In the early weeks of summer, clouds move constantly overhead. At night, thanks to the Saharan dust cloud, the intensely pink and violet striated sky is a reminder of the world that still, in theory, exists beyond the walls of our house, even past the edges of this city, which I rarely venture into--leaving the house only for doctor's appointments, the ultrasound wand sweeping over my growing belly. When the sky goes dark before a storm, it resembles nothing so much as the roving darkness I see on the ultrasound screen, revealing the inside of my body and the stranger growing there, heartbeat already tumbling. He looks so far away, like he could be pulsing on another planet, some distant moon.

At my first ultrasound, when the technician asked if my husband and I had been *trying to conceive,* I realized this word still seemed relegated to the world of thought, to concepts I could or could not grasp. Conception itself seemed like a far-off idea I hadn't quite wrapped my mind around. I never thought pregnancy would feel so alien; this new world growing inside me, without stopping to let me know. Before I got pregnant, when the idea of a child was faraway and abstract, I worried about what kind of world a child would grow into and inherit: hotter, for sure, and either wetter or dryer, I couldn't say. Less predictable, I knew. But those changes, too, seemed somewhere in the future, at arm's length. I didn't know the world could go strange so quickly.

The world inside my body is strange, too: at another ultrasound appointment, months later, the technician tells me the baby is transverse. "He'll turn soon," the doctors and nurses reassure me, but he doesn't, and at night I lay in bed hoping to feel him move into place.

When I sleep, I dream of friends and family confessing to me that they've gone to a party indoors, or quit wearing masks, or that they have a fever. I wake in tears, feeling that nothing can be trusted—not the world's patterns, or the people I love, or my own body changing as it forms this new life, hell-bent on entering the world sideways.

There are fleeting moments in *Doomsday Preppers*, in which the life of a prepper does not make me physically recoil: the misty backyard gardens, the gleaming vegetables sealed in glass jars, the bleating, weird-eyed backyard goats. But by the end, things always turn dark: The family suits up in camouflage for military-style drills, pulling out sniper rifles, or unleashing a torrent of boulders to block a road, or setting bear traps along property lines.

Doomsday Preppers debuted in 2011 as the highest-rated show on the National Geographic channel, but it was canceled after only four seasons, as concern grew about the implications of giving a platform to apocalyptic weapons enthusiasts and conspiracy theorists. A year into the show's run, in 2012, a young man shot his mother as well as twenty children and six adults at Sandy Hook Elementary School. Reports circulated that his mother was a prepper, that she worried about economic and social collapse. Her son used three of her five guns to slaughter schoolchildren.

The theory held by most preppers seems to be that, in the event of some massive calamity, cities would quickly dissolve into chaos, and city dwellers would flood the countryside, stealing resources from the better-prepared, more self-sufficient rural population. This was the consistent binary: preppers (and rural populations more broadly) relied on themselves, while people in cities relied on other people. City-dwellers relied on farmers to grow their food, truck drivers to keep grocery shelves stocked, and stores to keep their pantries full and their panic at bay. Doomsday preppers anticipate apocalypses of all kinds, where the world as we know it disappears and society breaks down. In these secular visions of apocalypse, though, preppers turn not to God but to themselves. Their self-sufficiency is what saves them. In *Notes from an Apocalypse,* writer Mark O'Connell describes the prepper movement "as a hysterical symptom of America itself." He writes, "Preppers are not preparing for their fears; they are preparing for their fantasies."

It is difficult to separate prepping from white supremacy. As preppers describe their expectations of the fallen world to come, they consistently invoke "rioting and looting," predict angry masses in the streets, stores and businesses smashed and emptied, before these depraved, city-dwelling crowds eventually turn on each other, raiding their neighbors' kitchens and gardens. Anyone preparing for this kind of future, O'Connell writes, was "never fully convinced by the idea of society in the first place."

"To be a prepper," O'Connell concludes, "was to do everything one could do to avoid being one of the sufferers oneself, while contributing nothing to the prevention or alleviation of suffering in others." Preppers failed to recognize that "it was precisely society's most marginalized and oppressed people who truly understood what it might mean to live in a postapocalyptic world, and who were therefore most fully prepared," O'Connell writes. The failure of preppers to acknowledge this reality revealed "a total moral incapacity."

Preppers take drastic measures to disappear, to seal themselves off and protect their own resources. Some of them "bug out," retreating to secret locations. Our pandemic life looked much more like "bugging in," prepper parlance for retreating, not to a far-off isolated bunker, but deep into one's own home: metal screens cover the windows, the family moves into their basement or underground bunker, they close the door behind them, and wait.

As the month we expected to be confined to our home stretches to two months, then three, then six, the world shrinks down, from the city we once moved through, to the walls of our house. At night, I lie in bed on my side, my mind strangely blank, with Colin curled up behind me, his hand on my belly. The baby kicks, and the world grows somehow even smaller: contracting from this house we barely leave, to the four corners of our bed, to our two bodies and this third, mysterious one we've just begun referring to by name. I wanted a wider world for him. He kicks; we gasp, then laugh. The world shrinks down again.

In the Bible, preparing for the "day of the Lord" is often compared to preparing for a home invasion. Matthew 24:43 says, "If the homeowner had known in which watch of the night the thief was coming, he would have kept watch and would not have let his house be broken into." Similarly, 2 Peter 3:10 warns that "the day of the Lord will come as a thief in the night, in which the heavens will pass away with a great noise, and the elements will melt with fervent heat; both the earth and the works that are in it will be burned up."

The comparison seems to be that, just as a homeowner protects his home against a burglary, even though he does not know if or when he may be robbed, so should the faithful prepare for the end of the world, even though they do not know when that day will come.

Peter continues: "Since everything will be destroyed in this way, what kind of people ought you to be?" Left open-ended, this seems like the central question posed by whatever apocalypses we anticipate: In the face of destruction, who should we be? How should we live? Should we hunker down in our basements, prepare ourselves for global collapse? Should we do everything we can to avert calamity?

But this scripture continues, answering its own question: "You ought to live holy and godly lives as you look forward to the day of God and speed its coming. That day will bring about the destruction of the heavens by fire, and the elements will melt in the heat. But in keeping with his promise we are looking forward to a new heaven and a new earth, where righteousness dwells." *Look forward to the destruction,* this scripture tells us. *Speed its coming.*

In the first few weeks of my second trimester, disappointed about a canceled trip to the mountains, my husband and I decided to camp out in the backyard. We pitch a tent, cook hot dogs over the fire, eat s'mores while the cicadas tune up for the evening, screaming in the trees. We crawl into the tent as the sky eases toward dark, and are lying in the (relative, cicada-filled) quiet for only a moment before sirens begin wailing all around us, a chorus of police cars, ambulances, fire engines in every direction. We don't say anything at first, but after a few minutes the cacophony has become absurd. "Is it always like this," we ask, laughing, "every night? Or is the world ending right now?" Lying right next to each other, we have to raise our voices to be heard over the noise. I never hear the sirens end, fall asleep lulled by the constant drone.

I don't want to identify with preppers, with their fantasies of surviving, tucked away, while the world burns. But in the weeks after I first heard the baby's heartbeat whirring on the Doppler machine, I felt some new, internal urge pulling me toward the world.

Six months pregnant, I walk restless laps around the backyard, digging tiny trenches and tossing handfuls of seed at the saturated ground—zinnias, sunflowers, and marigolds, as well as flowers I'm certain can't grow here, in this heat—delphinium, bells of Ireland, hollyhocks. Every morning, I can't help but check to see if there are any over-zealous seedlings, the way I check my own body for new signs of the other life I carry inside of me.

I think of preppers while reading the Gospel of Thomas, a mysterious and apocryphal collection of Jesus's sayings that I turn to often for some paradoxical clarity: "Prepare yourself with great strength, so the robbers cannot find a way to get to you, for the trouble you expect will come. Let there be among you a person who understands."

On first reading, these verses seemed to echo other scriptural warnings about being prepared for the end of the world. But one line stands out to me, pops back into my mind as I begin to fall asleep at night: *The trouble you expect will come.* It could be interpreted as an instruction to prepare for the worst, or it could be a reminder to be wary of self-fulfilling prophecies.

Maybe whatever we imagine will be "unveiled" in the apocalypse depends on what kind of world we imagine lurks just beneath the surface of the everyday. Preppers might expect the unveiled world to be a place of violence and tribalism, where each man must fight for himself. Those who believe in the rapture, or in Christ's second coming, might anticipate that the unveiled world will be a place of depravity and sin, and that a new, better world awaits them. I have always hoped that any unveiled world might reveal a hidden wholeness.

Perhaps the doomsday you imagine reveals nothing of the world itself, or its future, so much as it reveals your own fantasies and fears:

The trouble you expect will come.

Let there be among you a person who understands.

"We live in a time of looming," O'Connell writes, "of things impending and imminent." But ours is not the only or the first of such times. Each age comes with its predictions of the end, with its sense that the present moment must be somehow penultimate. I find myself collecting these lines, from across the centuries, predicting impending doom.

Saint Augustine, in the fifth century, reflected on the apocalyptic fervor of Christ's earliest followers, three hundred years earlier: "Those were the last days then; how much more so now!"

Fourteen centuries later, from one French novelist to another,

George Sand wrote to Gustave Flaubert: "What an age! Every one is dying, everything is dying, and the earth is dying also, eaten up by the sun and the wind."

Lurking beyond or behind these anxious predictions lies what might be the initial impulse toward apocalyptic thinking; the end of the world each of us carries in our own bodies. Over each day's frustrations, banalities, and tiny joys, the hovering awareness that one day the stage lights will drop for good and everything we've loved will cease to be.

When I was a kid, I was fascinated by the end. Lying in my parents' bed, I'd try to imagine what it would feel like to be dead. *No seeing,* I'd think, pulling the covers over my head. *No hearing*—I plugged my ears with my fingers. *No thinking,* I'd think. *No feeling the texture of the blanket warming my skin. No warmth at all.* Then I'd pull my fingers from my ears, push the blankets off my body, and sit up, gasping for air.

Augustine decided that nothing about the end could be known. He defined his present moment—somewhere between God's entrance into the world in the incarnation and Christ's second coming—as the *saeculum,* from which we get the word secular. Augustine believed that the faithful should be prepared for the end, but should not neglect their daily lives, their present moment, in anticipation of it.

"I don't know where I get the courage to keep on living in the midst of these ruins," Sand continued. "Let us love each other to the end."

Maybe I am wrong to be suspicious of prepping. Maybe I've conjured too dark an image for an impulse I can, in fact, understand—to keep yourself and your loved ones safe. But I find myself thinking in binary terms, separating the impulse to prepare for another world from the impulse to repair the world we have. While 'prepping' seems to require pulling oneself from the present in order to focus on the future, the work of repair requires living in a present that is deeply invested in the future. Repair might be a way of building a future without leaving the present behind.

At the end of each segment of *Doomsday Preppers*, a voiceover narration debunks each of the scenarios we've just watched preppers expound upon at length, detailing the way they would survive a massive flood, a terrorist takeover, a breakdown of the US agricultural system. The narration waves away each of their concerns. Financial collapse? "Most economists do not believe the United States is currently at risk," the narration says. But the voice never declares self-sufficiency a myth, never debunks the mindset of prepping itself.

It's possible to think of Noah as the original prepper: building a floating bunker, storing up food, making plans to save his family and sail away when troubles came. Jericho Vincent, the rabbi of Brooklyn's Temple of the Stranger, teaches Torah to thousands of Instagram followers, of which I am a devoted one. Vincent's series, "The World's Oldest Book Club," explicates the Torah from a mystical, queer, and justice-oriented lens and tends to send me racing for my journal to jot down notes about some story I've read a million times.

In one of Vincent's posts about Noah, they write, "Noah is introduced this way: 'Noah was a righteous person, he was at peace in his generation; Noah walked with God.' Sound like a hero? The third century Talmudic master Rabbi Yochanan says no. Only in his generation, Noah was a righteous person. In any other generation he'd be judged much more harshly. A truly righteous person would have figured out how to save other people's kids, not just his own."

These ancient stories are a warning, Vincent argues: "[I]f we only look after ourselves, we will ultimately be betrayed. Survival of our loved ones is not enough." It is not enough to save our own children from the flood, Vincent argues. "We must figure out how we're all going to ensure that all children survive the flood."

In some ways, the pandemic resembles the bleak future preppers have imagined. The *New York Times* reports that, according to one poll, about 44 percent of likely voters in the U.S. "see the coronavirus pandemic and economic meltdown as either a wake-up call to faith, a sign of God's coming judgment or both." The pandemic lays bare the stark divides between those with access to healthcare and those without; between those, like me and my husband, who can work from home, and those who are deemed essential enough to go to work and risk illness and death, but not essential enough to pay a living wage.

In the early days of the pandemic—in what we thought might be the later days, but which, in retrospect, turned out to be the early days—there is a lot of discussion about who's at risk, who's not at risk; who has antibodies and who doesn't; and how these categories could be used strategically. But these categories assume we live in distinct bubbles, in which people who are not at risk do not come into regular contact with those who are; in which people do not move through these states fluidly themselves. In real life, there are no such boundaries. Either none of us is at risk, or we all are.

Pregnancy is, similarly, a lesson in the body's permeability. I sit up too quickly and can feel the baby's tiny hiccups ricocheting against my belly. I am careful with what I eat, aware of the risks to the other life growing inside me, but aware, also, of the impossibility of creating a "pure" environment; microplastics have been detected in placenta and in breast milk; this new life will, for better or worse, live in the world just as I do. In the first year of the pandemic, hiding away inside our home, with our first child forming in my womb, I felt totally incapable of ensuring that my child—not to mention anyone else's—would survive whatever flood was already heading our way. And more convinced than ever that this was the task of our time.

If we had been blind to our own privileges before, the pandemic unveiled them in the revealing glare of its spotlight. The first aid kits Colin made and placed in the trunks of our cars were promptly stolen by "a thief in the night" who needed Band-Aids and blister packs of ibuprofen. In whatever future remains, I am sure I will think often of the summer I spent pregnant, in a global pandemic, in record heat, floating in my parents' above-ground pool, while someone, somewhere—I knew with absolute certainty—was dying of thirst.

The eschatological visions of our changing climate show many apocalypses, not just one; bespoke ends of the world shaped by factors like geography, race, and income level. Memphis may not be in danger of hurricanes or wildfires, but projections show the county where I live is at high risk of extreme heat in the coming years. And in our first years back in Memphis, winter storms hit harder every year, too. In the middle of the interminable summer of my long, lonesome pregnancy, I could not have imagined the ice storm that would hit Memphis when my son was five months old. Single-digit temperatures, no electricity, frigid winds whistling through our drafty old windows. There was a boil order for the city's water supply, and I'd just quit pumping, so we spent hours nervously boiling water to make formula for our five-month-old baby.

But we survived—a white, middle-class family in a majority-Black city with high levels of poverty—spending long days gathered around my parents' fireplace, sleeping in layers of clothing and knit hats, the generator working to keep one radiator heater running in my son's nursery while I laid awake in the next room, listening for each of his barely audible breaths.

Within these same city limits, older and poorer people froze to death on park benches, or in their own homes. In Texas, the same storm knocked out the power grid, leading to hundreds of deaths from hypothermia, carbon monoxide poisoning, and previously existing health problems that were exacerbated by the storm. In Jackson, Mississippi, the storm shut down the local water treatment plant, leaving Jackson residents without water for a month, and with many boil advisories in the months that followed.

Heat is what I'd always feared for my hometown, for my region. This fierce cold—and our crumbling infrastructure's inability to respond to it—unsettles my sense that I could ever know what's coming. In whatever future we are headed toward, it seems the ability to escape each coming calamity will be measured not by the ability to see it coming, to prepare for it—but by brute degrees of privilege and luck.

I find alternate visions of the apocalypse—and how to prepare for it—everywhere I seek them out. In "How to Survive the End of the World," a podcast hosted by writer adrienne maree brown and her sister, Autumn Brown, adrienne's first piece of advice for surviving the apocalypse has nothing to do with bunkers or plans for escape. Instead, she suggests the first thing we should do is get to know our neighbors. On her blog, brown writes, "Maybe apocalypse means going to the precipice of new life, and transforming my relationship to the world from being solely responsible for myself to being completely responsible for the well-being of another, of others. that kind of apocalypse sparks curiosity more than fear."

And there are glimpses of another, possible world, everywhere I look. Our younger neighbors pick up groceries for the older ones. We leave food in new community fridges behind churches and community centers. Local mutual aid networks ensure elderly people make it to doctor's appointments, and that poor people remain fed.

Prepping and mutual aid could potentially be seen as two sides of the same coin, two opposing reactions to the same impulses and fears. Prepping, with its deep distrust of the government, assumes that when society inevitably collapses, only the resilient, resourced individual and his family will make it out alive. Mutual aid shares a similar distrust of government, and sees communal networks as a way to resist state systems that are built to protect privileged few at the expense of the collective. But where preppers are often focused on saving their individual families, mutual aid networks seek to create new communities of care and support that can function apart from systems that so often serve to alienate us from each other.

"You picked a great time to have a baby!" a former professor laughed, sarcastically, on the phone when we told him we were expecting. But throughout endless weeks of suffocating, hundred-degree heat, I found deliveries on our doorstep nearly every day: bundles of curly purple kale from a friend's garden; banana bread fresh from my sister's oven; a thank you card from our elderly neighbor who'd lost her husband and her son to COVID-19 in the same week; a book that a new friend suggested I should read; a potted plant from an old friend on the other side of the country; a baby blanket from a neighbor who'd just heard our small piece of good news.

Six months into the pandemic, perhaps unwisely, we quit watching *Doomsday Preppers* and switch to *Alone*, a reality show in which contestants are deposited, alone, into a vast wilderness, and compete to outlast each other. They rig up complicated fishing apparatuses and build mossy huts. They talk to themselves a lot. When a wolverine begins stealing one man's stash of moose meat, he hacks the wolverine to death. At the end, he recounts this with breathless awe as he embraces his wife: "I killed a wolverine," he says, incredulously. "With an ax."

Colin and I joke that, after six months stuck together inside our house, every minute of every day, *Alone* has become a kind of fantasy; to be so ensconced in solitude that your own voice is a kind of company. Within my own body, for those long months, I was never alone. I laid down and felt a small someone adjust himself against my ribs. I ate and the person inside me got hiccups. For the first time, the trinity's strange imagery made a kind of sense: I was at once one person, and also two—myself, and somehow more.

After months isolated in our house, my growing belly the only sign that time is, in fact, moving ahead as usual, I discover that I can't think farther than a week or two ahead. For the first time in my life, I find myself spending an hour at a time sitting totally still, staring at the ceiling or out at the greening backyard, with a hand pressed to my side. An app on my phone keeps track of my pregnancy and tells me, each week, how big the baby is now: a blueberry, a kiwi, a cucumber. At the top of the app, I have the option to click ahead to view future weeks, to see what's coming next. But I never do; even in this small way, it feels impossible to try and imagine the future with any kind of wider lens. I am incapable of thinking of anything so abstract as a future, or a world, or what it might hold, or how I might prepare for it.

Two days before my due date, I write in my journal about our long, thrice-daily walks around our neighborhood. The neighbors assess my growing belly. "You about ready, Martha?" our one-hundred-year-old neighbor Maureen cackles from her front porch as I waddle by. "She looks done," Susan tells my parents. Jeff, the lawyer training to be a Greek Orthodox priest, runs out one morning as we walk by to give us his favorite baby book, a set of muslin swaddles, and his usual blessing: "God bless you and your baby."

Three days after my due date, in the waning hours of August, we wake to debris scattered across our yard, up and down our street, tree limbs and trash blown in by a storm. South of us, hurricanes sweep the coast. Preparing for a likely induction, we drive in misting rain to the hospital for a COVID-19 test. I find myself wishing I'd asked for a later induction date, but also wishing not to wait any longer.

"I wouldn't want to be born this summer, either," my friend Eileen texts me, when I complain about all the waiting. That week: another Black man shot by police, this time in Wisconsin; two protesters killed by a baby-faced teenager with a semi-automatic rifle; a hell-scape of a Republican convention; a hurricane south of us and wild-fires to the west. I imagine our son gripping the walls of my body, refusing to come out, and I can't blame him.

When John received his vision for the end of the world, alone on the island of Patmos, he heard a loud voice "like a trumpet" sounding behind him. He turned to see an angel, who said, "Write, therefore, what you have seen, what is now and what will take place later." So John wrote.

In his book of Revelation, John's singular, first-person pronoun works as a quote from God, as when he says, *I know your deeds,* or *I am coming soon.* Other times, John returns to narrating his vision, and speaks as himself again: *after this I looked, and there before me was a door standing open in heaven.* In these moments, I can imagine him saying, *hey, this is just what I saw. I didn't come up with this stuff. I know this sounds loony.* As he addresses each of the churches he's been commanded to write to, he repeats the refrain, *Whoever has ears, let them hear.*

What John tells them—and us—is that after heaven and earth pass away, a new heaven and earth come to take their place. John's book doesn't end in an underground bunker, or an urban wasteland, or even a green, rural paradise. Instead, John sees a new city descend from heaven. Angels take their time measuring all the proportions. When Revelation ends, there is no lone survivor, no winner, no prize, except a God that John swears will wipe every tear. No small feat.

Four days after my due date, our old brown hound, normally so aloof, reaches peak anxiety, eyeing me warily at all times. I have to lock him out of our bedroom at night or I'll trip over him, lying on the floor in the dark, always as close to me as he can get. In the morning, bleary, I walk around the garden, small concentric circles growing tighter, looping in on themselves, my swollen feet wearing paths to who knows where.

There is a new motion in my own body, sudden and insistent, not at all conceptual. In the backyard, tiny green shoots appear from the wet ground like a miracle, like something totally mundane. All these small signs of this world yet to come.

THIS IS PARADISE

IN THE GRAINY 1972 televised interview, Elvy Edison Callaway's back is curved over a polished wooden cane. He wears a white fedora, professorial eyeglasses, and the thinnest dusting of a white mustache. When he's not talking, his mouth moves continually, as if eager for another chance to speak. Callaway, a lawyer, former Baptist minister, and failed one-time Florida gubernatorial candidate, had spent the last two decades trying to convince anyone who would listen that he'd made a monumental discovery. While combing through Genesis, he'd looked around northern Florida and noticed the ways the local topography—even the flora and fauna—seemed to match up perfectly with the descriptions of the Garden of Eden that he found in the text.

"The Bible gives us certain definite facts," Callaway wrote in his 1966 book, *In the Beginning*, "corroborated by nature, science, and other unimpeachable evidence, which conclusively proves that the Garden of Eden was located east of the Apalachicola River, between Bristol and Chattahoochee, in Liberty and Gadsden counties, Florida."

Just like the river described in Genesis, the Apalachicola flows east. Callaway observed four rivers that connect with the Apalachicola and concluded that the Flint River was once known as the Gihon; Spring Creek River was the Euphrates; the Chattahoochee River was once called Pishon; and Fish Pond Creek was once known as the Hiddekel, or Tigris.

The river could have been just a coincidence, but when Callaway read about the gopher wood that Noah used to build the ark, he thought it sounded a lot like the Florida torreya, what locals called the stinking cedar, a small subcanopy conifer that grew in the steephead ravines along the Apalachicola River—and nowhere else in the world. When Callaway unearthed three petrified gopher wood logs, each of them twenty inches in diameter and six feet long, he knew what he'd found: "They were cast off from the building of the Ark," he wrote.

In Callaway's version of the Great Flood, Noah and his family floated down the Apalachicola and out to sea, drifting for 150 days, until landing in Turkey. "Noah and his family did not know that they had landed on Mt. Ararat, so far from their original home in Liberty County, Florida," Callaway wrote.

After Callaway made his discovery, he built a roadside attraction, with billboards along the highway counting down the miles to the Garden of Eden. Callaway's Garden of Eden was open to the public by 1956. Visitors paid $1 plus 10 cents tax to walk the trails overlooking the Apalachicola River. Black-and-white promotional photographs show families walking winding paths beneath hand-painted signs marking *the Birthplace of Adam; the Site of Adam and Eve's First Home; Where God Discovered Adam Was Lonely; Where Noah Made the Ark of Gopher Wood.* Today, The Nature Conservancy maintains that land as scientists, conservationists, and landowners work—sometimes with conflicting approaches—to preserve and protect the Florida torreya, one of the world's rarest trees.

In the 1830s, an amateur botanist named Hardy Croom was wandering along the banks of the Apalachicola when he noticed an unfamiliar tree growing in dense groves on Aspalaga Bluff. "A tree from 20 to 40 feet high, and from 6 to 12 inches in diameter. It grows plentifully, on calcareous knolls," he wrote in 1834. Croom took samples and mailed them to the botanist John Torrey, who determined that this tree was an entirely new genus of conifer. Croom suggested the tree be named after Torrey. Decades later, at Torrey's funeral, members of the Torrey Botanical Club brought cuttings from a torreya tree and laid them across his coffin.

In his 1875 essay "A Pilgrimage to Torreya," Torrey's student Asa Gray, who would later be referred to as the father of American botany, wrote that very few botanists had seen the torreya growing in the wild, and he "was desirous to be one of the number." Even Torrey himself never saw one in the wild, though he traveled to Florida in 1872, a year before his death, and saw a Florida torreya growing in a garden in downtown Tallahassee. Two years after Torrey's death,

Gray planned to "make a pious pilgrimage to the secluded native haunts of that rarest of trees, the Torreya taxifolia."

When Gray arrived in the Panhandle, he found few specimens, and the ones he saw disappointed him: "I saw no tree with a trunk over 6 inches in diameter," he wrote. He returned to the steamboat as night fell, bringing with him a bundle of torreya seedlings, hoping that one of them might be planted at Torrey's grave. On the return voyage, the steamboat passed Aspalaga Bluff. Only half a century had passed since Croom had first seen the torreya growing there, but Gray noted that Aspalaga Bluff was bare; the plentiful torreyas that once lined its banks had been cut down and used as fuel for steamboats like the one carrying him upriver.

This might have been the first major blow to the torreya population; in the years to come, they would be harvested and used as shingles, fence posts, and Christmas trees. By the middle of the 20th century, torreyas were further threatened by a mysterious fungus. Today, ailing trees are still unable to sexually reproduce; instead, they send up spindly shoots from the ground—none of which reach maturity. The fungus covers their thin, stunted trunks in cankerous sores.

Lately, increasingly severe—and frequent—hurricanes and tropical storms might be the biggest threat to the torreya. Though the torreyas themselves are often left standing in the wake of a storm, they depend on the shade of the canopy and are scalded by direct sunlight when larger trees fall. According to a report from the University of Florida's Institute of Food and Agriculture Sciences, the Florida torreya has declined a staggering 99 percent from an estimated population of 357,500 in 1914 to approximately 1,350 in the 1990s. Today, the torreya's population has dwindled to an estimated 400 to 600 trees.

In 1885 the botanist A.W. Chapman published an essay about the Florida torreya in which he seems to consider the tree already on its way out: The torreya "is destined," he wrote, "to ultimate extinction."

"For some reason, it's difficult to be impassive about trees," Jordan Kisner writes in an essay on the quaking aspen. "Since the Tree of Life, a mytheme common to ancient religions from every corner of the world, we have been telling stories about trees to tell stories about ourselves, and so it's hard to resist our desire to make the tree a story, to make it our story, to make it us."

Before I ever saw a Florida torreya, I felt a strange kinship with this tree that seems so chronically out of place, unsuited to its habitat, and which for decades now has been unable or unwilling to reproduce. Whenever my husband and I imagined our future children, I made constant, silent, mental calculations, visualizing our child's lifespan alongside scientists' projections for warming temperatures, rising seas, and stronger, more frequent storms.

Scientists estimate that the Florida torreya has existed for 165 million years. In its ancient age—and its current precarity—the torreya seems emblematic of deep time as well as our present moment, when the change that humans have wrought, in our relatively short existence, threatens the survival of many similarly ancient species.

Today, the Florida torreya is at the center of a debate between conservationists and local landowners, and between those who favor restoring the tree in its native habitat and those who advocate for assisted migration, or manually evacuating the tree farther north. A group called the Torreya Guardians has been working to plant torreya seeds and seedlings in states such as Michigan and New Hampshire, in hopes that the tree might fare better in cooler climates. Their "free-planting experiments" involve planting seeds directly into forests—mostly onto their own land.

Advocates of assisted migration argue that the torreya doesn't have time for the painstakingly slow approach of native habitat restoration favored by most scientists and conservationists. Opponents worry that there are too many unknown implications for directly moving a tree species beyond its native range, but the most immediate concern is that assisted migration could introduce the fungus attacking the Florida torreya to other vulnerable tree species.

But the disagreement seems to extend beyond the scientific argument itself, to a place that's more abstract and ideological. One environmental journalist I spoke with likened the Torreya Guardians to climate change deniers, and said she refused to include their perspective in any of her stories. If she sided with the science, she said, why would she include those that choose to ignore it?

When I talked to one leader advocating for assisted migration, she warned me that the controversy surrounding the Florida torreya was too big and too messy to write about, too contentious. She wouldn't speak on the record. "I am very wary of journalists," she wrote, adding that I was "walking into a bullfight to pet the bull." She added, "Unless you want to invest hours and hours learning about the Endangered Species Act, climate change, assisted migration, the paleohistory of glacial relict trees, and the intense politics of this issue, do choose something else to write about." She signed her email, "For the future."

But whenever I tried to put the torreya out of my mind, I thought of Callaway's rewriting of Genesis on the land around him. Callaway is often portrayed as a prototypical "Florida Man," a wacko preaching a brand of off-kilter biblical literalism. But lately, I've felt drawn to places where people like him have sensed something sacred, where the space between heaven and earth—and time itself—seems to grow thin. I've wondered what it might mean, in an era of environmental collapse, to look for the divine in nature. Perhaps more than anything, I've been compelled to see what I might learn from a tree that hovers somewhere between the past and the present.

I was three months pregnant when I planned a trip to the Panhandle. I would leave on March 20, 2020, stay in the White Squirrel Inn in Quincy, Florida, and finally see the torreyas in person. Of course, you know the rest. A week before my scheduled trip, the coronavirus was declared a global pandemic, and I emailed cancellations and apologies, promising that I would make the trip during maternity leave. I could not conceive of the pandemic lasting as long as September or October. I tried to think positively, envisioning hikes with a sleeping infant strapped to my chest. I'd heard the forests in which the torreya grew were among the few places in Florida where the leaves change color in the fall.

When Trey Fletcher was growing up in the 1980s, fearful of impending nuclear war, he always imagined he would retreat to Torreya State Park "when the shit hit the fan." Trey knew the park well; there was clean water in abundance, and he could hunt for food and hide out in the forest's deep ravines and lush vegetation.

Trey grew up in Gadsden County, Florida, hearing about the Florida torreya, an otherwise ordinary tree that was central to the story that had defined his hometown for over half a century. As a child, Trey saw Callaway's book, *In the Beginning*, displayed prominently on the bookshelf at a friend's house, and wondered often about the author's theory that the Garden of Eden was just a few miles down the road.

He told me many of the people he grew up around couldn't necessarily identify a torreya, but they all knew the myth: Adam and Eve once made their home here along the Apalachicola River, and Noah had used the wood of the Florida torreya to build his ark.

Trey left home to study interdisciplinary ecology at the University of Florida. When people asked him what he wanted to do with his master's degree, he told them he wanted to go back home, to work to preserve that particular environment. Now Trey works as a horticulturist and curator at the Atlanta Botanical Garden (ABG), which houses the largest collection of Florida torreyas outside of the trees' historic natural range.

It made sense that, as a child anticipating the apocalypse, Trey would have thought of Torreya State Park. According to Callaway, the torreya had helped humanity survive before. Surely the tree could do it again.

"But the apocalypse," Trey said, "got to the park first."

When Hurricane Michael hit the Panhandle in 2018, Trey's sister called from Gadsden County, where she lives in the house their great-great-grandfather built 150 years ago. She was frantic; the rain was coming through the walls. As soon as the roads opened, Trey drove home, checking on his mother and sister before heading toward Torreya State Park. Trey made it as far as Aspalaga Bluff before being blocked by debris.

"The giant trees that had lined the road were all knocked down," Trey recalled. "The air was redolent with the smell of tree sap. Ancient trees had been ripped up and cast like matchsticks into the bottoms of ravines."

Trey said he had expected he might cry, or scream, or tear his hair out when he saw the devastation the hurricane had wrought. But when he arrived, he said, "It was overwhelming. It was too much. It was just a void."

Trey was one of several people I talked to who would begin to tell me about their property, or their favorite hiking trail, and only half-way through seem to remember—as if shocked from a bad dream—that this place no longer exists, at least not in the way they remember it. Trey would shift from the present tense to the past, correcting himself as he recalled the ways Hurricane Michael had changed the landscape, perhaps irrevocably.

In our conversation, Trey was careful to steer clear of the controversy surrounding assisted migration, but he says he would like to see the torreya restored in its natural habitat. Although he was quick to note that he holds the accepted position of the scientific community, it seemed that Trey's support for native habitat restoration comes from a more personal place: "I'm from there," he said, "and I have such an affection for the place. I'd love to see the tree restored in that environment."

The Atlanta Botanical Garden keeps a "safeguarding collection" of Florida torreyas, as well as cryogenically stored seeds in its Gainesville, Georgia, facility. ABG staff monitor their torreyas in hopes that some of the trees will prove resistant to the fungus. These could then be crossbred, boosting the trees' resilience against the invasive fungus that has plagued them for over half a century.

Much of Trey's connection to the torreya felt serendipitous to him: "According to the myth," he said, "Noah supposedly built the ark out of the Florida torreya. And now we've essentially built an ark for these trees at the Atlanta Botanical Garden."

In early 2018, a group of ABG staff members took a field trip to Torreya State Park. Even though Trey worked with succulents and desert plants, he went along as a local, a translator of sorts. The group spent their time putting up fencing around torreya trees to keep deer from rubbing their antlers on the trees' spindly trunks, causing damage and further spreading the fungus that has been killing the trees for decades.

It had been years since Trey had walked the trails at Torreya State Park. He thought back to the summer of 1998, when he'd decided to come out to himself and to a few close friends, but not yet to his family. He was feeling "a lot of distress" when he decided to go on a solo camping trip in Torreya State Park. He hiked out to Rock Bluff Campground and sat in a tree overlooking the Apalachicola River.

"I sat and watched the sun go down, watching the moonlight on the river," he said. "I thought about the decision I'd made, and I wondered where it would take me, how it would change my life."

Trey told me he often thought back to that moment, looking out over the Apalachicola River, when he knew that his life was about to change. One afternoon during the trip with other ABG staff members, twenty years later, Trey hiked out by himself to the same campground in the late afternoon sun. He stood there, watching the foam rise in the river below.

"I realized I'd found at least part of the answer to the question I'd asked myself, twenty years before," he said. His decision to come out, to be himself, "led me right back to that same place, doing what I'd always wanted to do, which was to help preserve it."

But landowners on the Panhandle are often wary of the work of conservation organizations. Some keep the torreya trees on their land a secret, to avoid attracting attention or because they believe the government might take their land away. In Trey's roles as both a scientist and a local, he hopes he may be able to heal some of the divides between the scientific community and the local landowners, whom he sees as crucial allies in the fight to save this tree.

Trey told me about meeting with a group of scientists and locals in a restaurant just outside Torreya State Park. It was a hole-in-the-wall place with no sign outside, and Trey found himself seated between the two groups, serving as a kind of translator for each side.

"It's a cliché you hear all the time," Trey said, "that to get people involved in conservation you have to make them feel like you care about them. But I'm not just trying to make people feel like I care about them. I actually do. Yes, I'm interested in the trees and the conservation efforts, but I'm also interested in the people themselves."

"As an ecologist," he said, "you get called a tree hugger a lot. But ecology is ultimately about people; helping people deal with the changes that are coming."

For as long as humans have written about the Florida torreya, it's existed only along a small stretch of the Apalachicola River. But the tree likely grew farther north until the Ice Age, when glaciers pushed the torreya, and many other

species, south. When the glaciers retreated, the Florida torreya was left behind, trapped in cool, shady steephead ravines for the last 10,000 years.

This theory explains the presence of other plants, like mountain laurel and flame azalea, that are found in this area of the Panhandle, even though they typically live in the higher elevations and cooler temperatures of the Appalachian Mountains. Proponents of assisted migration argue that the Florida torreya's true native habitat is much farther north than a tiny stretch of the Florida Panhandle. The trees are not able to migrate fast enough on their own, they say, and are stressed by an increasingly warm climate.

When Chris Larson and her husband, Robert, bought their 115-acre property in Mossy Head, Florida, now called Shoal Sanctuary, twenty years ago, the land had been deforested. Since then, the Larsons have worked to cultivate a diverse forest, planting 14,000 trees so far, including fifty redwoods and dozens of Florida torreyas.

"Assisted migration is necessary," Chris Larson told me right away, the first time we spoke.

The Larsons, who consider themselves affiliates of the Torreya Guardians, are two of many volunteer planters growing torreyas on private land. On the Torreya Guardians' website, these volunteers catalog their efforts in incredible detail, comparing plants grown from seeds or cuttings; in flower pots or coffee cans with the bottoms cut out; watered with irrigation systems or "ambient rainfall"; surrounded by mothballs or nibbled by groundhogs.

In her book *Rambunctious Garden,* environmental writer Emma Marris wrote that the "conundrum" of assisted migration has "paralyzed" scientists: "Proponents of moving plants and animals threatened by rising temperatures to more hospitable locations are more concerned about the increasing rate of species extinction, while opponents are more worried about the integrity of coevolved ecosystems. But in general, scientists are pretty freaked out by the whole idea."

The Torreya Guardians website acknowledged that "the concept of assisted migration will directly conflict with established conservation principles." But, they argued, "the risk associated with doing nothing is greater than the risk associated with intervening." Hurricane Michael added some urgency to their work. To the Larsons, moving the torreyas north might be the trees' last hope for survival. But they also seemed like an example of negative capability: cultivating torreyas on their land in the Panhandle, while advocating for other volunteers to help move the tree farther north.

Online, the Torreya Guardians seem to practice an almost religious devotion to the torreya, posting photographs of each plant, documenting their halting progress over the years. They excitedly note good luck planting torreya seedlings alongside ginger root. Sprouts emerging from rodent droppings are hailed as "miraculous."

The first time we spoke on the phone, Donna Wright told me about the day she went to see a piece of property that was for sale in Gadsden County. She stood on a high ridge and looked down over a creek, its sandy banks winding off into the distance. "I just couldn't believe that I could own something that beautiful," she said. Shortly after she purchased the land, Donna's friend, a biologist, came to see it and identified several torreyas growing on the property. Soon Donna was hearing from the Florida Native Plant Society, the Atlanta Botanical Garden. Scientists wanted to see her trees.

At first, Donna was enthusiastic about cooperating with scientists. She even delayed a scheduled double mastectomy to meet with the Atlanta Botanical Garden representatives in February 2010: "I scheduled the procedure around their visit because I thought, 'Well, if I miss this, I might as well be dead,'" Donna said.

ABG staff members walked Donna's property and took samples of her trees. She told me it is hard to describe what a moving experience that was, but she soon began to feel disillusioned. "The group gets bigger, committees take over, and soon I'm a long way from the scientists themselves."

All of the torreyas on Donna's property showed signs of the fungus that is wiping out torreya populations across their tiny range. But, she said, the trees are beautiful.

Donna and I had been emailing for a few weeks by the time she finally agreed to speak with me. For Donna, the controversy surrounding the torreya is fraught, and deeply personal. Donna's mother died from breast cancer, and Donna's experience as a survivor of breast cancer is intimately linked to the trees she cares for: Florida torreyas often grow alongside the Florida yew, which contains taxol, a compound used to treat breast cancer, as well as other cancers and diseases. Though she cared for these trees—her voice often broke with emotion when she talked about them—Donna chose to distance herself from organized conservation efforts.

"People's appreciation for this tree is woven into their being," Donna said, "and then, in come the scientists, and it's two different worlds. If I were doing this work, I'd go to a landowner and ask them why they love the torreya, why they find meaning in it. People here get so frustrated with conservationists. When they hear 'conservation,' they close the door. I have had to back up, to maintain the sacredness of it all, the joy, and quietly know that I've kept the torreyas safe. I'm still keeping them safe," Donna said. "And my reward is that I get to be alone in the woods with a plant that's on its way out. Not everybody gets to do that."

Road access to Donna's property was blocked for years following Hurricane Michael. Across Donna's thirteen-acre property, the hurricane toppled many of the larger hardwoods, depriving the smaller torreyas of their protective shade. After the hurricane, Donna began training her German shorthaired pointer, Tucker, to sniff out torreyas that might be trapped under debris. Donna predicted her torreyas might be scalded by the increased sunlight. But when she talked about her land, even in its damaged state, she said, "God lives there. When you're in the woods, everything behaves as it should."

When I asked Donna what she thought about the local lore, that the Garden of Eden was located not far from the thirteen acres that are so sacred to her, she said, "Well why not? Why not? If you get out of the literal interpretation, the whole thing's very lovely. Isn't that the beauty of faith, that we have this gap? It's like a lot of Christian apologetics will try to prove God, even though the Bible says you can't. There's a chasm there, between what we know and what we don't, and the chasm is faith."

Donna told me she often weighs conservation efforts against the threat of climate change: "Maybe we're helping a little bit," she says, "but the earth is going to recreate itself through climate change. By not participating in organized conservation efforts, I haven't hurt a thing. At all."

I wasn't sure how I felt about Donna's resistance to cooperating with scientists who had the resources and devotion needed to protect these trees. It seemed that the privilege of owning land came with its own weighty responsibilities. Places like Florida are among the most vulnerable to the effects of climate change. Coastal areas are threatened by rising seas, while increasingly destructive hurricanes have wreaked havoc on coastal and inland areas alike. Relatively few people have access to the kind of financial—and sometimes physical—security provided by land ownership, and the land Donna owns, with its population of torreya trees, comes with the opportunity to play an active role in the future of a critically endangered species.

When I asked Donna about her role as a landowner in this work, she paused for a moment. "I don't know that any of us own land, really," she said, "but we pay a lot of money to shoulder the burden of stewardship. And in that way, the trees are under my stewardship for right now. And the sense of responsibility or love is deep. It's almost intimate. I walk in the woods and I walk past them and for now, for now, they're mine. I have this little teeny window." Her voice wavered. "My ownership of this land will be so short when you compare it to all of time. But for right now they're mine."

An Apalachicola riverboat captain named Gill Autrey told me that he first heard about E.E. Callaway from a mysterious passenger, a woman who kept her signed copy of *In the Beginning* wrapped in aluminum foil and held it with gloved hands. Autrey tracked down a copy for himself, and he told me that the book made him a believer. "You mean to tell me the Garden of Eden was in Iran or Iraq?" he laughed. "Give me a break."

I asked Gill if he knew anyone who had been there when it was the Garden of Eden.

"Well, it still is," he said, sounding befuddled. "It still is the Garden of Eden."

At first, I thought he meant that the Garden of Eden tract had been preserved, that the 3.75-mile Garden of Eden Trail still winds its way along the bluffs there, much as it did during Callaway's time. But later, listening back to the recording of our conversation, I realized that wasn't what he meant. I'd betrayed my skepticism with the use of "was," that past-tense verb. My question, of course, implied that the Garden of Eden "wasn't" any longer.

In the opening pages of *In the Beginning,* Callaway uses the past and present tenses to introduce his subject: "The Garden was and is a fact, and was and is located between Bristol and Chattahoochee, Florida..." Callaway's language suggests the Garden of Eden has some essentially inherent, unchanging nature, which I heard from so many of the locals who spoke with me: a sense that the land they lived on was special, magical, somehow set apart.

Like Callaway, I grew up a preacher's kid in the South, though with a very different kind of religion. In my father's faith, the Bible was understood symbolically, or poetically, but not literally. I grew up thinking of the story of Adam and Eve's banishment from the Garden of Eden as a metaphor revealing humanity's essential feeling of alienation, from both God and the natural world.

But in Callaway's version of Genesis, paradise was not some distant, perfect land, guarded by angels with swords of fire, and it was not a mere metaphor, either. It was a real place, just down the road, that anybody could visit. There is a particular moment of Callaway's televised interview that I've replayed on YouTube dozens of times. Sitting on the bluffs overlooking the Apalachicola River, the sunlight glinting on the broad stretch of water churning behind him, Callaway made a proclamation: "I've studied the Bible and walked these woods, and I can prove that this is paradise."

Adam and Eve might have been banished from the Garden, but

the rest of us were not, so long as we could accept that paradise might not be some faraway idyll, but the marred, imperfect ground beneath our feet.

In the long list of plants and animals facing similar challenges and dwindling numbers, it might seem hard to justify the amount of attention and resources that the Florida torreyas command. Focusing on one ailing species often feels like a choice to ignore another. Compared with the Florida yew, with its cancer-fighting potential, or the gopher tortoise, whose deep, winding tunnels protect other species fleeing fires, it's hard to know what the Florida torreya offers—what it means—other than its role in a story projected onto it.

I've wondered how Callaway's story, of the torreyas' role in ushering the Earth's creatures to safety from the Great Flood, might have shifted meaning in today's context, when the tree is just one of many species that now need saving—from rising seas and rising temperatures, increasingly frequent and dangerous storms, melting ice and degraded soil.

When I first began researching Callaway, I often encountered depictions of him as a man ahead of—or at least very out of step with—his times. There were accounts of Callaway working as a lawyer for the NAACP, and running for the governor of Florida as a Republican when the state leaned heavily Democratic. There were stories of Callaway's grandfather emancipating the enslaved people who worked his land. Callaway described his father as "a farmer and Justice of the Peace, was also for 67 years a Baptist minister."

Callaway, too, seemed to contain multitudes. Born in Weogufka, Alabama, the son and grandson of Baptist ministers, Callaway left the church after refusing to repent for attending a dance. And though early in his life Callaway fell in love with the discoveries of scientists like Charles Darwin and Thomas Edison (Callaway's namesake), he struggled to reconcile that love with the religious conversion he experienced in his later years.

When I tried to get a sense of Callaway's life, I spoke to Marilyn Ray Smith, whose father was Callaway's first cousin and lifelong friend. Smith, who has lived in Boston since the 1960s, saw the Harvard biologist E.O. Wilson, another Alabamian with a passion for the environment and storytelling, as a vision of who Callaway might have become under different circumstances.

"Elvy had a very active, fertile mind and no place to go," Marilyn said, talking to me by phone from her home in Boston. "History books are full of people like this, who live in isolated communities, who don't march to the same drum, who have differences, and they often end up being quite eccentric. And so the neighbors think they're crazy. But you know what? He wasn't totally crazy."

The Garden of Eden was "a spectacular spot," Marilyn said. Because of Callaway, it had been saved.

It took me months to track down copies of Callaway's books, and what I found in them was not so much an exceptional mind but a more commonplace racism. His 1930s book, *The Soul of the South,* is dedicated to Southerners who sided with the Union in the Civil War, but argues that Black people and white people are fundamentally different and should not commingle. In that book, Callaway advocates for the full education for Black southerners, but primarily because he saw them as "such carriers of venereal disease."

Callaway's later book, *In the Beginning,* which I finally accessed from a Georgia library using interlibrary loan, might begin with Callaway's claim that the Garden of Eden "was and is located between Bristol and Chattahoochee, Florida," but the text that follows is peppered with political digressions and semi-hysterical rants about the evils of communism. Callaway credits the country's "racial strife" to "the miserable failure of organized religion," describes the serpent that appears in Genesis as a "welfare statist," and offers a strangely feminist interpretation of the story of Adam and Eve: "I am glad she ate [the forbidden fruit] and that she insisted upon Adam eating it as well. I am glad American Eves have insisted on their husbands and sons eating it ever since."

Perhaps Callaway's Garden of Eden theory was not a spiritual vision, but an earthly one, the fruit of a white American Christianity that has drifted so far from its origins that it would worship a blue-eyed Jesus and see America as God's chosen people. Perhaps Callaway, like Gill, the riverboat captain, simply found it impossible to imagine the Garden of Eden "in Iran or Iraq"—preferring, instead, to make the mental leaps required to situate the origins of humanity closer to home.

There were several proposed developments for the Garden of Eden site, including a Garden of Eden–themed amusement park, but none of them stuck until an anonymous $1 million donation allowed the Nature Conservancy to buy the land in 1982. Today the Garden of Eden tract makes up about 20 percent of the 6,295-acre Apalachicola Bluffs and Ravines Preserve. The ABRP sits on Garden of Eden Road and maintains a hiking loop through the original land maintained by Callaway. At the trailhead, a simple metal sign states "Garden of Eden Trail."

Few of the preserve's visitors know Callaway's history, says David Printiss, the Nature Conservancy's north Florida conservation manager. "That's ancient history, as it were."

At the Apalachicola Bluffs and Ravines Preserve, conservationists are focused on restoring longleaf pine habitat and preserving species-rich slope forests and seepage streams. When the Nature Conservancy began its work in the Panhandle, much of the land they'd purchased was badly damaged through heavy industrial treatment, but the Garden of Eden tract, because of its history as a roadside attraction, was relatively unscathed. Nature Conservancy staff were able to collect seeds in the Garden of Eden tract that helped restore the rest of the preserve, as well as the neighboring 13,735-acre Torreya State Park. David said he thinks of the Garden of Eden tract as "the Garden of Eden of longleaf pine diversity."

David told me that the steephead ravines in which torreyas typically grow are why the Nature Conservancy came to this area of the Florida Panhandle. But where they've really made a name for themselves, he said, is in restoring the uplands through prescribed burns, reintroducing fires that are an integral part of the forest's health.

Before so much of Florida was overpopulated, paved, and developed, Florida landscapes experienced frequent fires, due to lightning strikes and the management of indigenous peoples. Many species in the longleaf pine ecosystem, in particular, depend on regular fires in order to thrive. In 1990, Florida passed the Prescribed Burning Act to encourage controlled burns, particularly on privately-owned land, and Florida remains a leader in fire management on public and private lands. But this might not be enough to keep up with the larger effects of the changing climate.

On the ABRP website, photos documenting the damage done by Hurricane Michael show roofs ripped off of offices and classrooms; shade cloth hanging loose from the wiregrass nursery; volunteers picking up bits of insulation scattered across the preserve. Along the Apalachicola River, photos show nearly every tree ripped clean of leaves. Two years later, in 2020, the Garden of Eden Trail was one of the few trails reopened to the public.

"In many areas the torreyas are now underneath ten feet of debris," David said. "In geologic time, hurricanes would have come through here and the trees would have been able to sustain that. But they're highly stressed; they're not reproducing."

When I asked David how climate change might alter this area, he said, "Some things are obvious: sea level rise, things are going to be underwater; but others are like, what's it going to do to fire return intervals and soil moisture?"

For organizations like the Nature Conservancy working to restore native habitat, the torreya is just one of many endangered species that make up the larger ecosystem; here, there are also gopher tortoises, eastern indigo snakes, Florida pine snakes, Apalachicola rosemary, the Florida yew. Meanwhile, the very idea of restoration feels fraught: How do we restore a habitat to an ideal image of its past, while the future of that habitat seems increasingly uncertain?

Over the summer of 2020, Donna would send me emails every so often, checking in. "All good?" she asked in July. In August, she wanted to know what colors we'd chosen for the nursery. She had never been very social, she wrote, but after months of isolation she was officially lonely. She'd cordoned off a separate area of her house where her kids and their friends could stay on brief, distanced visits. "I cook for them," she wrote. "That feels like heaven." She asked me to keep her updated. A moment after her email arrived, my inbox chimed with another one: "And we'll meet eventually," she wrote. "Under a torreya tree."

By the time my son was born in September, I should have learned how little faith to put in my plans for the future. But I was surprised to give birth in a mask; surprised by how quickly we abandoned our birth plan; surprised by the emergency Cesarean section, my arms outstretched on either side of me, held down by my husband and the anesthesiologist while I shivered uncontrollably. I was surprised when I contracted an infection and spent weeks receiving daily antibiotic infusions while wearing a wound VAC. I was surprised when I found myself unable to walk around the block, much less travel, and I had to cancel the second trip I'd planned to meet the torreya in the Panhandle.

When I wrote Donna to let her know I'd have to cancel my trip, I attached a photo of my infant son, wrinkled and tiny in his hospital-issued hat. Donna responded with photos of her torreyas, their green needles shining in the sun. They seemed like all the world I could not get to, conjured up in a single image.

When I finally saw a Florida torreya, over a year after my originally scheduled trip, it was not in Florida at all, but in Asheville, North Carolina. In 1939, the botanist Chauncey Beadle gave several Florida torreya specimens to the Biltmore Estate. When my husband, my son, and I were driving back to Memphis after a family trip, we stopped at the Biltmore and wandered the expansive grounds, looking for a tree I'd never seen before. Walking through the fifteen-acre azalea garden, I flipped constantly between the paper map we got at the entrance and a screenshot of a hand-drawn map I found on the Torreya Guardians website, big red X's marking each torreya on the property.

The torreya we finally found stood near a pond, its limbs rustling in the cool mountain breeze as tourists walked by, unaware of the tree's plight, the arguments it inspired, or its precarious hold on the future. The torreya was larger than I'd expected: In 2015, the Torreya Guardians surveyed the torreyas growing at the Biltmore, and recorded diameters of forty-six inches and forty inches for this tree's two trunks, much larger than the trees, all less than six inches in diameter, that Asa Gray recorded on his 1875 trip to the Panhandle.

My husband stood on the path, our six-month-old son bundled into a carrier on his back, while I circled the tree, touching its bark and its gleaming needles. Before I became pregnant with my son, I worried constantly about my future child inheriting a diminishing world; when I looked around me, all I could see was loss. But once he was born, once he became not a future possibility but a present-day fact, I began to see these unpredictable ways—non-adherent to any baseline or ideal—that creatures find to thrive.

I took a handful of torreya needles in my palm. Their aroma, which I'd often read described as astringent, smelled more like celery than turpentine to me. This torreya, so far from its native range, looked healthy, unmarred by fungus or disease; it looked right at home.

When Donna and I first started talking, she didn't want to be identified by name. She was a private person, she said, and her experience navigating the disagreement surrounding the torreya had dissuaded her from associating herself with it publicly. When a photographer traveled to Florida to make pictures for the story, Donna and I talked about how he could take photos that obscured her face. But in the end, she posed for photos alongside her torreyas and allowed me to identify her. "You may certainly use my name," she wrote in one early morning email. "I am who I am: I am a conservationist. I consistently make decisions that conserve my land and everything on it. I stay away from conservation groups in general; I find they contain pockets of ambition, and a homogenous thinking that interfere with my joy."

Months after I began talking to Donna, she received a mailing from the Florida Native Plant Society, sent out to many landowners like her, asking if scientists could come survey her land and collect samples from her torreyas. Donna thought, "I'm going to wait for them to call me," and tucked the mailing away. Weeks later, they finally called, and Donna began to slowly welcome some scientists back onto her land. I asked Donna what had changed her mind. "They bridged the gap," Donna said.

Six months or so after my essay about the torreya was published, Donna and I caught up over the phone. I was sitting in a pool of sunlight on my bed while my son napped in the other room. Donna tried to describe her hesitancy to take part in the local conservation groups that had reached out to her since we last spoke. "I could have joined them, Martha," she said. "But I would have to be a different person."

"Donna!" I said, laughing. "I've never heard someone so clearly articulate the problem of my life."

After conversations with Atlanta Botanical Garden staff, she decided to donate a parcel of her land as a conservation easement.

Though Donna will retain ownership of the land, the Atlanta Botanical Garden will hold the easement. As part of the legal agreement, Donna has restricted access to her land so only her family and ABG staff may enter. I was surprised that Donna had been willing to cede so much control to an outside group. But I remembered, too, that when I first reached out to her, she only agreed to talk to me because I wasn't interested in pitting one "side" of the conflict surrounding the torreya against the other. She'd agreed to talk because I wanted, instead, to get to know her and her love for these trees. I told her that she seemed to have opened up a lot since we first started talking. Over time, Donna said, her heart had softened. She apologized: she knew that the new legal agreement meant I'd never see her torreyas myself.

In the coming months, she'd be footing the bill for an attorney, for several detailed surveys of her land, including a survey of every gopher tortoise hole on the property. She sighed as she recounted the litany of bureaucratic protocols and expenses. "I'm going to do this," she said. "Nothing is going to stop me."

There might not be much reason to hope for the recovery of a species like the Florida torreya—a tree most people haven't heard of, that has historically been confined to a tiny sliver of the country. But, in what is perhaps a sign of our dire times, people have begun to turn against hope anyway. In an essay titled "Beyond Hope," writer and philosopher Derrick Jensen writes, "Hope is what keeps us chained to the system, the conglomerate of people and ideas and ideals that is causing the destruction of the Earth." In a *New York Times* op-ed, "The Case Against Hope," writer and professor Roxane Gay writes, "Hope allows us to leave what is possible in the hands of others."

When I asked Donna whether she had hope that the torreya could make a comeback, she said, "My attitude with the torreya is that it's gone, unless someone can bring it back." In the end, she said, the tree's future is in the hands of the scientists at the Atlanta Botanical

Garden: "Its DNA is with them. Knowing this makes me feel a little bit eternal," she said. "The fact that science will bring this to fruition is a beautiful marriage to me, not a conflict; there's great faith on both sides." She was quiet for a moment. "Yes, I have great hope," she said finally. "I know something about tomorrow."

In my conversations with people trying to save the torreya, I noticed specific moments in which they seemed hopeful for the tree's future. But, perhaps more often, they seemed to do the work without much hope at all. Instead, the work itself was its own remedy against despair, against assuming that all was already lost. Talking to them, I began to get a sense of hope on a different scale, with an aperture opening beyond a specific tree's specific fate, perhaps something like what the writer Adrian Shirk calls "theological hope" which she defines as "not simply longing for Eden," but "a longing that is mobilizing, resistant, that leads us to each other, and maybe to a garden, even if it is a long way off."

This kind of hope moves beyond the survival of a single endangered tree, even perhaps our own individual survival, to a greater reconciliation. "All souls descend a ladder from heaven to the world," writes Abraham Joshua Heschel. "Then the ladders are taken away." If this is true, perhaps the goal is to quit looking around for another ladder, for our escape from this world to a paradise that we vaguely, achingly remember, and instead tend to the world around us as if it were—or could be—paradise itself.

What we witness now is not the end of the world but the end of many worlds, perhaps more worlds than we knew we had to lose: the world of the American chestnut, the whitebark pine, the maple-leaf oak, the eastern hemlock, and one day, perhaps very soon, the world of the Florida torreya. But as the torreya's extinction has become arguably more likely, people devoted to the tree have become less willing to admit it. They are compelled, instead, to build whatever arks need to be built.

THE TERMINAL SEA

IN 2015, THE UNIVERSITY of Georgia Press published *The Southern Frontier: Landscapes Inspired by Bartram's Travels.* The book included reproductions of more than sixty oil paintings by Georgia landscape artist Philip Juras, who aimed to replicate landscapes that the natural historian William Bartram would have encountered in the late eighteenth century as he journeyed through the South, documenting his findings in his famous book.

Bartram's *Travels* has captivated readers for his scientific descriptions and drawings of Southern flora and fauna, as well as his mystical descriptions of encountering the people and landscapes of Georgia, Florida, and the Carolinas. Juras writes that it is impossible to find Southern landscapes that perfectly represent the world Bartram would have seen: "Where a remnant does survive," he writes, "it is likely to have been greatly affected by fire suppression, hydrological alteration, and invasive species."

In one of the essays introducing his collection of paintings, Holly Koons McCullough, the director of collections and exhibitions at the

Telfair Museums, writes, "several of Juras's paintings represent not the splendid present or promising future, but the past—landscapes that will never exist again." In some instances, Juras had to recreate, whole cloth, places that have been entirely wiped off the map.

In his *Travels,* Bartram described the Keowee River Valley in the foothills of South Carolina as "a fertile vale, at this season, enamelled with the incarnate fragrant strawberries and blooming plants, through which the beautiful river meanders, sometimes gently flowing, but more frequently agitated, gliding swiftly between the fruitful strawberry banks." Today, the Keowee River Valley is submerged beneath a reservoir used by Duke Energy to generate electricity and cool three nearby nuclear reactors. For his painting *Keowee Valley,* Juras used archival photos and topographic maps of the area before the river was dammed and impounded to get a sense of the terrain. Juras photographed and painted nearby valleys in order to access "the more transient qualities of this imagined view."

Juras chose a spot in the Bon Secour National Wildlife Refuge to represent a beach where Bartram spent the night, camping as he made his way from Pensacola to Mobile. Juras writes, "I had to do some judicious editing in order to depict a scene Bartram would recognize." Juras left out "modern intrusions" like the heavy machinery that was stationed on the beach, working to clean up after the 2010 Deepwater Horizon BP oil spill in the gulf. The painting, *Gulf Dunes,* shows the chalk-white dunes of the Alabama coast, backlit by a gentle rosy sunrise, the gulf a sliver of golden light on the horizon.

"It is my hope," Juras writes, "that in presenting these important and often imperiled ecosystems in the context of the *Travels,* I might foster a greater awareness and appreciation of them and of the remarkable man who recorded this part of the world so eloquently more than two hundred years ago."

In choosing Bartram as the perspective to which Juras orients his work, Juras aims to show us what we've lost, in hopes that a glimpse of an unadulterated South might inspire viewers to protect, restore, and expand the remnant wild spaces that remain. But there is something about Juras's choices that nags at me, and I return to his images, and his descriptions of their creation, over and over. I wonder if it's right to edit out the machinery cleaning up an oil spill, or the bridge connecting two ends of a city damaged by increasingly frequent storms. Is this work an example of revision, or erasure, or a kind of repentance?

Bartram traveled as far west as Lake Pontchartrain, sailing twenty miles along the lake's north shore and observing dense marshes that stretched from the lake's shallows to the forests of the mainland. Juras describes Lake Pontchartrain beautifully, as "an in-between environment, a place where fresh water transitions to salt, where the Delta shifts subtly to the coast itself."

Today, Lake Pontchartrain is bisected by two twenty-mile-long bridges, built in 1955, that serve to connect the northern and southern ends of New Orleans. Satellite imagery shows the Lake Pontchartrain Causeway as a ghostly white line bisecting the murky expanse of water. Crossing the Lake Pontchartrain Causeway—the eerie sensation of driving over water with no land in sight—is a familiar experience to anyone who's traveled south into New Orleans. But in Juras's paintings, he leaves the causeway out. He writes, "If one ignores the long, thin line of the Lake Pontchartrain Causeway, as I have in *North Shore of Lake Pontchartrain,* it's not hard to imagine an eighteenth-century sailing vessel, no bigger than a speck in the distance, cruising off the marshy shore."

Using Bartram as a guide provides a helpfully limiting frame; rather than trying to depict the entire Southeast, Juras can focus his paintings on the areas that Bartram described in his *Travels.* But the frame is limiting—and limited—in other ways. The introduction to

Juras's book describes Bartram's *Travels* as "an ecological and environmental time capsule of the colonial South when it was still a relatively unknown and undocumented frontier." Unknown and undocumented, to whom? Juras's emphasis on Bartram's perspective on the "frontier" of the South often conjures the South incorrectly as a blank slate, uninhabited and unchanged.

One contemporary element did make its way into Juras's work. In 2005, Lake Pontchartrain was inundated with water following Hurricane Katrina and other tropical storms. *North Shore of Lake Pontchartrain* depicts some of this open water, in the middle ground of the painting, which would have been filled with grasses before the storms. Juras doesn't indicate why he included this ahistorical stretch of open water, but looking at the painting, I'd imagine it's because the open water between the marsh and the sky is a useful compositional frame. Unlike the machinery cleaning up after the oil spill, this contemporary feature of a damaged landscape is aesthetically pleasing; it can stay in.

Writing about the coastal marshes he encountered in the Southeast, Juras invokes Sidney Lanier, a nineteenth-century Georgia poet, whose poem "The Marshes of Glynn" was memorized by countless Georgia schoolchildren for generations. Lanier's poem is credited with introducing landlocked Central Georgians to their state's coasts: "Oh, what is abroad in the marsh and the terminal sea?/ Somehow my soul seems suddenly free/ From the weighing of fate and the sad discussion of sin/ By the length and the breadth and the sweep of the marshes of Glynn."

In the 1960s, when the Kerr-McGee corporation requested to lease 25,000 acres of coastal marshland for a phosphate mine, Georgian scientists, politicians, activists, and residents began to campaign for increased protection of Georgia's marshlands, often invoking Lanier's work—and "The Marshes of Glynn," in particular.

I read about one political cartoon from the time that showed Lanier hastily scribbling the last lines of "The Marshes of Glynn" while being scooped up in a bulldozer. In 1970, these advocates' efforts resulted in Georgia's Coastal Marshlands Protection Act.

As I write this, Georgia's Okefenokee Swamp, the largest blackwater swamp in North America, is threatened by a proposed strip mine. Twin Pines Minerals, an Alabama company, would mine for minerals such as titanium dioxide and zirconium, a process that would require the company to pump 1.4 million gallons of groundwater every day from the aquifer beneath the swamp, threatening an already drought-sensitive ecosystem.

As the "length and breadth and sweep" of southern coasts continue to be threatened by development, extractive industry, and rising seas, I wonder if we should return our souls to "the sad discussion of sin," to examine our wounds and our deprivations more closely.

Sometime in the past year or two, Instagram's algorithm guided me toward The Bible for Normal People, an organization that provides Biblical interpretation in short snippets via a podcast, Instagram account, and community programming. In one video, Jared Byas, a former pastor and professor, describes sin as a metaphor that changes over time. In the Hebrew Bible, metaphors describing sin change from a weight that one would need a beast of burden to carry, to a stain which could be cleansed in purification rituals. "As economies develop and we enter the world of the New Testament," Byas says, "sin becomes a debt that must be repaid."

Byas argues that the single unchanging aspect of sin is that it brings harm or breaks relationships between people and God—and between people and other people. What that harm looks like, and how it can be repaired, can change, along with our conceptions of sin, from one generation or one culture to another.

I like the idea that our metaphors for sin change as the world changes. Perhaps our contemporary era, defined as it is by exploitation and extraction, is changing our conceptions of sin—and repair. Perhaps, rather than editing out what we've done here, we should instead bear witness to a South plundered by extractive industry and exploitative labor, damaged by a mindset that would see this place as ever having been an "unknown and undocumented" frontier.

As I've spent time with Juras's paintings, I've thought often about pentimento, the term that refers to the presence of first drafts and abandoned images underneath a painting's finished surface. Some of these pentimenti are visible only under infra-red light and X-rays, but some appear, plainly visible to the eye, as the layers of paint grow thin over time. Pentimento is Italian for repentance, and pentimenti offer an understanding of repentance that goes beyond reflexive guilt or impotent apology: repentance as a fresh attempt, a new start. Repentance as the background upon which our lives are built.

Perhaps Juras's "judicious editing" is intended to point us beyond our fall from grace. Perhaps his landscapes—influenced as they are by history, memory, and imagination—are a way of allowing images of the past to call us forward, toward the necessary work of repair. But in oil painting, pentimenti are defined by the visibility of the past—of failed attempts, previous versions, and mistakes that guided the painting to its finished form.

Juras's landscapes, by contrast, might be defined by the invisibility of the past: the final images we see are stitched together from scraps, but no seams are left visible. The finished surface erases the distance between the unspoiled primordial forest that once was, and the strip mall we might see in its place.

People don't always see Southern landscapes as beautiful or inspiring. Our gentle foothills are less majestic than ice-capped mountains; our in-between places like bayous and marshes are less appreciated than the clarity of a rocky, windswept beach. Looking at Juras's paintings, I've felt moved by his depictions of these places that have so often, and for so long, been abused and exploited. But I have also felt that these depictions seem incomplete. A surface this smooth reveals none of the stitching Juras has done, and also betrays none of the textures of human history.

When I think of the landscapes I encountered growing up that most shaped my perspectives on the South, it's the scarred, patched-up places that return most readily to my mind. Pass Christian, Mississippi, where a hurricane opened up a Wal-Mart near the coast and left its contents strewn onto the beaches and into the surf; couches bobbing in the tide, clothing hanging from every gnarled tree. Or a small town in West Virginia, which locals referred to as "the end of the world," where houses clinging to hillsides were painted with leftover highway paint; white walls and yellow trim radiating the sunset's pink light. Or the West Tennessee church camp I attended each summer, on the edge of a massive, manmade lake; I could never look at it for long without imagining all the houses submerged under the water's still surface.

Looking at Juras's paintings, I find myself craving to see each place he depicts as it is now. I want to see the oil rigs ghosting the horizon, the heavy equipment cleaning up a spill, the damaged shoreline, the invasive species, the drowned valley, the power plant. I look at these images conjuring the past and feel an inward desire to flip the page and see how each place has transformed. There is a gap between Juras's work and the world, and I want to cross it.

When I think of more holistic landscape representations, I think of Keris Salmon's mixed-media work. Her 2016 series, "We Have Made These Lands What They Are," couples her photographs of Southern landscapes and plantation architecture with archival text. "Cargo" shows a heron with outstretched wings paired with text describing enslaved people who managed to escape. "Sugar" pairs a photo of a stately tree with text describing a fourteen-year-old enslaved girl's attempt to mix sugar with poison.

On her website, Salmon writes, "I am personally drawn to this material as black woman married to a descendant of the largest American tobacco plantation in the ante-bellum south, home over centuries to at least 447 enslaved people." Her work overlays surviving landscapes and architecture with historical texts, making the presence of the past in the world around us impossible to ignore.

Or I think of Xaviera Simmons's photographs. In one 2018 photo, a Black person stands in the center of a rocky landscape, holding a large handwritten sign that reads A COUNTRY BUILT ON FREE LABOR. In "On Sculpture #2," the background is a placid sea; the foreground is disrupted by the artist's hands holding up a black-and-white image torn from a book, showing people leaping from a boat. In both images, the physical landscape is necessarily disrupted by its context, by history made contemporary by virtue of its visibility.

In one interview, Simmons said, "Now I'm not sure about how to engage the landscape and be successful at it. I have to go back in and think of it with a sense of future. I don't want to hang on to past tropes."

Georgia, Juras's home state, was founded as a kind of utopian experiment in 1733 by James Edward Oglethorpe. In Oglethorpe's vision of Georgia, slavery was outlawed (as were lawyers, liquor, and Catholics). The state of Georgia, Oglethorpe believed, would achieve social equality for all its inhabitants through walkable urban design and wealth redistribution. Needless to say, Georgia fell far from Oglethorpe's vision: by the end of the Civil War, more enslaved people and slaveholders lived in Georgia than in any other state in the deep South.

"Art, we might argue, is by its very nature utopian," Erik Reece writes in his book on utopian societies. "By its very nature, art asks us to think in a different way about the realities we take for granted every day. It is a separate world, a contained world, an intensified world. The aims of art tend to be aspirational, even if they get filtered through a negative dialectic..."

However far it falls from its intentions, utopianism is necessarily future-oriented. Juras claims he wants his work to inspire habitat protection and landscape-level conservation across the South. But Juras's paintings do so by pointing backwards, aspiring to a past image of the places he depicts. Sometimes this past image is closer to the present-day state of the places he paints, other times the places themselves are long gone. But the idea of aspiring to any past image feels inherently nostalgic, and nostalgia for anything in the South is a poisoned well.

In an essay on Howard Finster, a very different Southern artist, the writer Garrard Conley describes an interaction he had with the novelist Garth Greenwell. As they drove through North Carolina, Conley remarked on the beauty of the houses they passed, and Greenwell said that, to him, the houses "looked like violence." Conley writes, "For some of us, nothing aesthetically pleasing in the South ever remains purely so. But if you view the world this way at all moments of your existence, the violence extends outward indefinitely and there is no sacred place on this earth, there is always some dark association ready to bubble up wherever you are. The question, for me, becomes not so much a moral as an existential one: How can we find joy and beauty in a broken world?" Perhaps the joy and beauty we find here must be essentially complicated—must be *made* complicated—in the art we make to represent it.

The Jewish tradition of teshuvah is often conflated with repentance, but its meaning is larger than any one individual's repentance for their sins. We arrive at the word "sin" from the Hebrew *chet,* meaning to miss the way or go astray, and the Greek *hamartia,* which derives from a technical term used in archery which literally means "to miss the mark."

While repentance is often associated with a feeling of guilt or regret, teshuva refers to an action in the world—in one's life—of returning to the path from which you've strayed. In his book *The River of Light: Jewish Mystical Awareness,* Rabbi Lawrence Kushner writes about teshuva as "a movement of return on a cosmic scale." Every apology, he writes, involves a "retreat from some territory thought conquered by the Self. Only now we understand that it did not belong to us and never did. And we 'return' to our place."

This is what I think of when I see Juras's paintings of Anthony Shoals on the Broad River, what Juras considers his "home river." Although there's something intriguing—even poignant—about Juras's process of research and reconstruction in order to represent landscapes of the past, his paintings of present-day landscapes, like Anthony Shoals, are, to this viewer, more emotionally charged. By which I mean, they make me emotional.

I've spent a long time staring at Juras's paintings of spider lilies growing among the rocks strewn throughout the river, with their soft white blooms glowing in the crepuscular light. Juras writes that very few populations of spider lilies survived the damming of the Savannah River watershed, and his paintings of these flowers blooming amidst the river rapids speak to the persistence of beauty in wounded, unlikely places.

Some of my favorite of Juras's paintings depict controlled burns, paintings he makes while suited up, standing at an easel, in the midst of a burning forest. These paintings, showing red and orange flames moving through the underbrush, sending up plumes of purple smoke, are sketch-like, full of movement, almost abstract in their effort to capture a constantly shifting, incandescent present.

ARKANSAS PROPHECY

I'M IN THE CAR'S backseat, listening to my mother and my aunt Lynn up front, talking about Jesus. We're driving through Arkansas to visit my great-aunt Connie. The fields outside the car are flat and wet from a three-day drizzle. My mother is saying she and Lynn are only Christian because their parents raised them in the church. She says if they had been raised in another tradition, another family, another place, somewhere outside Milan, Tennessee, that they might belong to a different religion now. To her, it's all in the raising.

Lynn seems to disagree but takes a long time saying so—like Jesus, Lynn tells stories instead of saying what she thinks. She tells about how her car broke down once, years ago, and she felt compelled to walk to the gas station, rather than the pay phone, to call her husband, and how on the way to the gas station she discovered a little girl standing all alone on the sidewalk. When Lynn asked the girl where her mommy was, the girl took Lynn's hand and led her to her house, where the girl had slipped out the front door while her mother was taking a nap.

"Now why did I walk to the gas station, to use their phone," Lynn asks, "rather than walk to the pay phone in the opposite direction?"

The question hangs in the wet air.

Lynn has recently joined a mega-church where she lives, in Kansas, and she thinks she might be the only Democrat in the congregation. After a long pause, Lynn says she's been told by her new minister that she has a gift for prophecy. We don't say anything to that, either.

Outside, the road is a blur of gray and yellow. Leftover cotton bolls droop from the plants, and birds fly in low clumps. The last time I saw my great-aunt Connie, she was living in her old house in Jonesboro with a white cat she called Charlie. She called everything *Charlie* when she forgot what it was really called—*bring me that Charlie,* she'd say, gesturing toward a deck of cards or a pair of knitting needles.

Connie is the last of seven siblings, the rest all dead from various cancers decades earlier. She's had cancer, too, many times, but has survived each round. The family theory about the cancer revolves around the cotton field they'd lived next to, the chemicals sprayed over the rows every year, the acrid haze in the air that they didn't know to stay out of.

A few years ago, on another trip to Arkansas with my mother and Aunt Lynn, Connie fixed us glasses of sweet tea, sat down with us on the patio, and told us she was ready to die. Everyone she loved most was dead, she said, and she felt left behind.

"I picked out the box already," she said. "Paid for it outright."

As if it were going to happen later that afternoon, Lynn said she wanted to be cremated.

"It's much better for the environment," she said, nodding to herself, and asked if Connie had considered it. Connie wrinkled up her face.

"My people don't do so good with fire," Connie said, before turning to my mother to ask if my father would perform her funeral. "Or does he know too much about me?"

That was three or four years ago. She's still waiting. She's still got the box.

I've seen an old black and white photo of Connie climbing into the cockpit of her husband's crop duster. She's looking over her shoulder, winking at the camera. In her wedding photos, she's wearing a suit jacket and a skirt, sauntering down the aisle, her hips cocked. I know she's been moved into a nursing home since the last time we visited, that we're headed to a place I've never seen, but as we drive I imagine her still in her own house, with her arts and crafts room and Charlie and her sunny backyard.

A couple days before our visit, Connie's son called to warn us that Connie was not always right in the head. To me, she had never seemed completely right in the head; that's why I liked her so much. Her Southern accent is clipped, whip-quick, hard to understand. At a surprise birthday party we threw for her a few years back, she referred to one of her best friends as *that size two bitch* and made my grandmother laugh so hard she cried.

Connie has another son she calls *troubled.* A few months ago, when he told Connie he was planning to kill himself, Connie said, "Honey, I'm over eighty years old, I can't deal with this right now. Do what you need to do."

Up front, my mother and Lynn are talking about how, on long drives, their parents used to pull over and let them pick cattails along the side of the highway, or stop to buy A&W Root Beer floats. My mother checks her memories against her sister's. My mother's memories are like mine—some obviously invented, some too blurry to see clearly, some mixed with dreams. Many of her memories and Lynn's do not overlap. Lynn remembers a neighbor's naked, featherless cockatiel. My mother remembers Lynn once stuck a whole pack of straight pins through my mother's mattress, sharp ends up. Lynn says she has no memory of this. She doesn't like to talk about it.

When we get to the nursing home we are led through a series of circuitous, identical hallways. Each door is decorated with an oversized Christmas wreath. We find Connie's apartment door wide open. We call her name and Connie appears, elf-like, tinier than ever. She's pointing to a trio of large, plastic figurines on her dresser.

"Look, these are for you," Connie says to my mother, pulling her close. They look at the figurines, Christmas carolers in red robes, their mouths open wide.

"They're moving," Connie says, "and they have fangs."

The figurines aren't moving, and they do not have fangs. Connie's face and throat are badly bruised from a fall she had a week ago. She shows us a digital picture frame her son gave her for Christmas. A photo of my cousins glows at us. Connie tells us we can email photos to her son and he can send them to the frame. That way, she says, she'll have more than one picture to look at.

"What kinds of pictures do you want us to send?" my mother asks.

"Obscene," Connie says, chuckling, and resumes searching for a missing sock, which she is calling *Charlie*. She seems agitated. She has two mismatched shoes—one blue, one white—waiting for her on the end of the bed. While Connie is in the bathroom, my mother finds the other blue shoe and places the lone white shoe back in the closet.

When Connie comes back from the bathroom, she gives up on the socks, sticks her bare feet into the blue shoes, and tells us we're going to the cafeteria for lunch. We head out into the hallway, walking so slowly I have to stop every so often and take a few steps backward so as not to leave the group behind. In the cafeteria, we sit at a corner table. There are salads and coleslaw waiting for us. There is throbbing pop music playing in the kitchen, but it seems none of the residents can hear it.

A sweet-looking old lady in a wheelchair pushes herself into the cafeteria. Connie turns to watch her roll past us.

"I know *her* reputation," Connie says, not bothering to lower her voice, "They can't hear anything," she explains, gesturing to the table next to us, where the old lady with the apparently dubious reputation has pushed herself up to a place setting and is unwrapping her plastic utensils.

"Maybe by Monday we'll have our days figured out," the little old lady offers up to the women at the table next to us.

"What?"

"Maybe by Monday," the woman repeats, "we'll have our days figured out."

One of the women still can't hear her, so the women pass the message around the table, like a loud game of Telephone. A woman with a walker makes her slow approach to their table. "Here I am with the crackers," she says. From her back pocket, she unfurls a handful of the same plastic-wrapped crackers we received with our salads. "Don't have as many as usual," she says apologetically.

"I'll take what you got," one of the women responds, taking the crackers and doling them out to the other women at the table. The first man I've seen all day shuffles out of the dining hall, telling everyone *buenas noches,* though it is not yet noon.

My mother studied Geriatrics in college, and throughout my childhood she worked for the Alzheimer's Association and Catholic nursing homes. Between my mother's nursing homes and my father's churches, I spent my childhood surrounded by elderly people. After school, playing in the empty dining room at the Alzheimer's Association, I listened to the old lady who walked laps while repeating, "All I ever get is junk mail and bills. All I ever get is junk mail and bills."

I asked my mother, once, if her experience with aging meant she'd make for an easygoing old lady. "Oh, no," she said, "I know all the tricks."

At our table, Connie looks suddenly excited, as if it's finally occurred to her that she has visitors, that today is different somehow. Her old mischievous expression returns, and I can see the woman I've known, the woman I've heard so many stories about. For a second she is the woman who, on a family trip to a wedding in New Orleans, took a troupe of female relatives along with her to male strip clubs, where she slipped dollar bills in the strippers' G-strings. She looks up at us. She has an audience.

"People used to see us together, me and your mama, and they'd say, 'oh look at that Juanita, she is so pretty.' And then they'd see me with my frizzy strawberry-colored hair and they'd say, 'where'd that one come from?'"

Connie laughs, but her face is shifting. It's like watching an actor change characters mid-scene. She seems suddenly far away, not quite here, anymore.

"I hid under the bed when daddy came home," she says. "If one of my school friends had come home to play with me, I'd make her hide under the bed with me. Do you know what daddy's last words were, to mama?"

We shake our heads, no.

"'*You think you're so goddamned smart, don't you,*'" she says, in a near-hiss. "Then he stopped talking at all, and then he died."

"Did he ever hit you?" Lynn asks.

"No, he never hit me or Juanita. He hit the boys and he pushed mama around. I saw the French doors rattle when she fell back against them."

We're all watching her now, her wet eyes focused somewhere beyond us, beyond this strange, green room and the bodies moving slowly around us.

"When he had a heart attack, your mama ran to get help," she says. "All the way across Shelby, Mississippi, Juanita ran and ran and prayed that her daddy wouldn't make it. She prayed that he'd die."

My mother and Lynn are nodding; they know this part of the story.

"She never forgave herself for that," my mother says, looking at her hands in her lap.

Before she got sick, my grandmother Juanita opened a charity secondhand shop in Milan, Tennessee, called the Mustard Seed. I've seen pictures of her in the newspaper at the groundbreaking for the store's second, larger building. Her head, bald from chemo, is covered in a flower-printed scarf. She mimes pushing the shovel into the dirt, but it is clear from her posture that her strength was fading.

When Juanita died she was sixty-two years old, a year younger than Lynn, and the same age my mother is now. My grieving mother was pregnant with me when she and my ten-year-old sister went to the grand opening of the Mustard Seed's new location. Decades after Juanita's death, when I was in high school, my mother took me to visit the Mustard Seed once more. I was surprised to see a large framed photo of Juanita on the wall; the same coiffed black hair and red lips I'd seen in all our family photo albums, beaming down from behind the cash register.

"I miss your mama," Connie says. "Why did she have to go and do that?"

By *do that* she means *die.* Time is fast-forwarding now in Connie's mind; past Juanita's running prayer, past the birth of Juanita's four children and her cancer diagnosis, all the way to the year I was born, the year Juanita died. Sometimes I think Juanita and I must have passed each other, in whatever murky space there is between living and not-living.

I feel a little guilty, overhearing these stories which seem to have been deliberately kept hidden from me, from anyone. Mostly, Connie speaks to Lynn and my mother as if I'm not there, anyway. When

Connie looks at me, I'm certain she doesn't know exactly who I am. But I have Juanita's eyes, my mother's brown hair, Lynn's upturned nose. Connie sees something she knows in me, so she tells her stories.

I know it's supposed to be sad, how time opens and slams doors in Connie's mind. But the way time moves for Connie seems also kind of beautiful. The years collapse, accordion-style, and stories she's never told appear unbidden and can't be held back. Maybe, I think, this is one of the gifts of the threshold Connie has waited so long to pass through. The veils fall away, the walls she's built up collapse; she can be her many selves, all at once.

In this space between living and not, Connie can let all those tightly-guarded memories loose. She can let someone else share the burden of all that pain: the rattling French doors, her shallow breathing under the bed, her sister's prayerful feet pounding the Mississippi earth. All that guilt. Connie is crossing over. She has the box. She is ready to make her appearance. Lord, she is ready.

In the beginning
GOD CREATED.
800-FOR-TRUTH

FOR THE LIVING OF THESE DAYS

IN THE BLANKETING HEAT of late July I found myself in a packed courtroom in East Tennessee, watching history repeat itself. The tiny town of Dayton has hosted a reenactment of the Scopes trial every summer since 1988, the year I was born. The annual reenactment cycles through five scripts: *Destiny in Dayton, One Hot Summer, Front Page News, How it Started,* and the version I'd come to see, *Monkey in the Middle.* I'd heard that other reenactments included musical numbers, bluegrass interludes. But *Monkey in the Middle,* the script selected for the summer of 2022, seemed to be a more literal interpretation of the trial, squeezing eight days of testimony and arguments, mostly verbatim, into a two-hour performance.

The 1925 "Scopes Monkey Trial," as it was dubbed by *Baltimore Sun* reporter H.L. Mencken, centered around a high school teacher, John T. Scopes, who was accused of teaching evolution to his high school students in violation of Tennessee's Butler Act. It was the first trial to be broadcast on the radio, and was cast as a fight to the death between opposing sides. It was not just that either defense attorney Clarence

Darrow or prosecutor William Jennings Bryan would prevail; in an era of polarized, symbolic politics not unlike our own, they represented a battle between the educated progressive and the Bible-thumping fundamentalist; the secular and the religious; the future and the past.

Today, the reenactment's vibe is decidedly unsanctimonious; on the festival logo, a smiling chimpanzee plucks at a cartoon banjo. But whoever wrote the copy for the Rhea County Heritage Foundation website seemed well aware of the trial's contemporary resonance, promising that the reenactment would rehash "arguments supporting Darwin or the Bible, majority or minority rights, parental control of schools, and much more."

The stately brick courthouse where the trial was held anchors Dayton's tidy downtown. On the eightieth anniversary of the Scopes trial, in 2005, a statue of William Jennings Bryan was erected on the south side of the courthouse lawn, where it stood alone, unchallenged, for over a decade. In 2017, Freedom from Religion, Inc. unveiled a statue of Clarence Darrow on the north side of the lawn, dedicating it on the first day of that year's Scopes trial festival. When I arrived, I watched people milling around, taking selfies with the two statues that stood, not quite facing each other, on the velvety green lawn.

I'd bought a ticket for the reenactment the day the box office opened. I wanted to know what meaning this trial held—and still holds—for Dayton, and for conservative white evangelicalism at large, and how that meaning has changed over time. I wanted to know what story Dayton is telling about itself, about history, and about faith as it reenacts this story every year. I'd intended to go to Dayton on my own, had purchased a mountain of trail mix expecting a quick drive there and back and a night alone in a motel. But just before my trip, my parents and I watched the 1960 film *Inherit the Wind,* a fictionalized account of the Scopes trial, and by the end of the movie they'd purchased their own tickets; they wanted to come along with me.

Inherit the Wind has always been one of my dad's favorite movies, which seems strange, given the way the film lampoons religion: In the opening scenes, the townspeople travel as a mob, belting "Give me that Old Time Religion" and holding signs with slogans like "Doomsday for Darwin" and "You Can't Make Monkeys Out of Us" as they march around town. But the religion represented by the characters in the movie bears no resemblance to my father's faith. In his coverage of the Scopes trial, the *Baltimore Sun* journalist H.L. Mencken wrote that a Methodist like my father "would be regarded as virtually an atheist in Dayton." Some things have not changed; my father enjoys seeing fundamentalist Christianity get whooped by a Yankee agnostic as much as the next guy.

In the courtroom, my parents and I settled onto the same stiff, wooden seats that had been present for the original trial. The floor-to-ceiling windows had been covered in heavy black fabric; stage lights hung from the ceiling. Once the room was full, the director came out and coached the audience: We would be responding to cues projected on a screen, prompting us to applaud, laugh, or murmur incredulously to each other. Our participation corresponded to audience reactions that had been recorded in the trial transcripts. With these instructions, the director took his seat, the actors appeared on stage, and the play began, with jury selection.

Every choice made while condensing a 336-page trial transcript into a script for a two-hour play seemed hyper-deliberate, muscular, like watching a sculpture emerge from a block of stone. On stage, the actor who (quite convincingly) portrayed Bryan questioned a high school biology textbook that categorized humans as mammals: "How dared those scientists put man in a little ring like that with lions and tigers and everything that is bad," Bryan bellowed. "These parents have a right to say that no teacher paid by them shall rob their children of faith in God and send them back to their houses skeptical infidels, agnostics, or atheists!" In the front row, several audience members' heads nodded in agreement.

As someone raised in a faith tradition that saw science and faith as compatible ways of understanding the world, I never truly understood why conservative Christians opposed evolution so stridently—the two sides, falling behind battle lines drawn long before I or my parents or my grandparents were born, seemed impossible to penetrate. But this moment, as Bryan held up a faded green copy of *Civic Biology* on the courtroom floor, illuminated a core aspect of the conflict that I had not previously understood: The Butler Act of 1925 did not prevent public school science teachers from teaching about the theory of evolution generally; teachers were allowed to tell their students that other animals had evolved from "lower life forms." The Butler Act specifically prohibited teaching that *humans* had evolved.

On stage, Bryan paced. He wanted to know: When, in that supposedly long and ongoing process of evolving, did people commit the original sin that propelled their fall from grace? And if people did not fall from grace, if there was no original sin, how did that change Christians' understanding of salvation? And if there was no salvation, what did that do to the Christian assurance of life everlasting?

To Bryan, proponents of evolution couldn't answer—or even meaningfully address—these profoundly disorienting theological questions: "They don't tell us where man became endowed with the hope of immortality," Bryan said. "They believe that man has been rising all the time; that he never fell from grace…" To Bryan, evolution was an alternate origin story that could not be integrated into the one around which his faith—his entire understanding of the world—was structured. The question of when man "shed his tail" and when he "acquired his immortality" were intimately related: If we are not the product of God's design, created by God in God's image, can we have *evolved* into God's image?

Next, the part of the trial I was more familiar with: Darrow had intended to call eight experts to testify about evolution, but the judge barred all but one, a zoologist, from testifying before the court. With all the experts for the defense deemed irrelevant, Darrow finally called Bryan himself as an expert on the Bible. The judge moved the proceedings out of the packed, stifling courtroom and onto the courthouse lawn, where 3,000 people (roughly three times the town's population at the time) gathered to watch.

In the trial transcript, these interactions look ready-made for a script, with the characters volleying back and forth. Darrow grilled Bryan on the age of the earth, the provenance of Cain's wife, and the precise date of the great flood. Bryan's time on the witness stand, arguably the most famous part of the trial as it persists in public memory, was included in the reenactment in a highly condensed form. His most infamous quote—*I do not think about things I don't think about*—was left out entirely.

When Bryan hedged that the six days of creation described in Genesis might not have been literal, twenty-four-hour days, but longer "periods," Darrow lunged:

Darrow: "If you call those [days] periods, they may have been a very long time."

Bryan: "They might have been."

Darrow: "The creation might have been going on for a very long time?"

Bryan: "It might have continued for millions of years."

Whenever Bryan appeared caught like this, there were periodic outbursts from the gathered crowd or attempts to stop the questioning. (We, in the audience, were prompted by the projector to turn to our neighbors and murmur the word "watermelon" to conjure generalized consternation.) On stage, the actor portraying Bryan insisted that Darrow continue: "The gentlemen have not had much chance—they did not come here to try this case. They came here to try revealed religion. I am here to defend it, and they can ask me any question they please." The projector screen hanging above the actors prompted us to applaud for Bryan, in accordance with the trial transcript, and we did.

Bryan's time on the witness stand ended abruptly, when the judge announced that court would adjourn until the next morning. The next day, the judge declared he would expunge the previous day's testimony from the record. This prevented Bryan from calling Darrow as a witness, though he did submit the questions he'd prepared to the press for publication. Scopes was declared guilty, and ordered to pay a $100 fine, a ruling that was later overruled on a technicality. The reenactment ended as abruptly as the trial itself: The lights came up, and we rose from our chairs and began our slow exit through the courtroom's double doors.

The audience spilled out onto the courthouse lawn, where the evening air had finally cooled. By the time I made it outside, most of the crowd had dissipated, threading through the town's quiet, half-lit streets. On the courthouse lawn, the statues of Bryan and Darrow stood alone, forced to spend every night together in silence, under the stars. Behind the courthouse, the foothills that had seemed far away in the daytime suddenly loomed, navy silhouettes under a sky pitched toward night.

By most accounts, the road to the Scopes trial began when John Washington Butler, a Tennessee farmer and member of the state House of Representatives, introduced a law that would prohibit Tennessee public school teachers from denying the creation story as it was found in Genesis and from teaching that humans had evolved from "a lower order of animals." Butler admitted that he "didn't know anything" about evolution, and had no evidence that Tennessee school teachers were actually teaching Darwin's theory in their classrooms. But he'd read in the newspaper "that boys and girls were coming home from school," he said, "and telling their fathers and mothers that the Bible was all nonsense." The Butler Act was swiftly signed into law without much fanfare. During the Scopes trial, Butler told reporters that he didn't expect his bill to "make a fuss." "I just thought it would become law, and that everybody would abide by it and that we wouldn't hear any more of evolution in Tennessee."

I'd wager the specter of the Scopes trial began to appear on the horizon years earlier, on a Sunday morning in May 1922, when Reverend Harry Emerson Fosdick stepped into his pulpit at First Presbyterian Church in Manhattan. Fosdick was small, with thin wire glasses and curly hair rising over a high forehead. Though he served a Presbyterian congregation, he had been raised a Baptist. In 1898, while still a college student, he wrote a letter to his mother about his changing faith: "I'll behave as though there were a God," he wrote, "but mentally, I'm going to clear God out of the universe and start all over to see what I can find." Years later, as Fosdick returned to his faith, he served as an Army chaplain in France in World War I. Later, he would change his stance on the United States' involvement in the war, and said he had been a "gullible fool." Fosdick was a person who changed his mind. From his pulpit, he addressed the unwillingness of a rising number of Christians—"the people who call themselves fundamentalists"—to do the same.

According to Fosdick, a "great mass of new knowledge" had come to light in the course of one generation—knowledge not only about the world and its natural laws, but also about human history. "[M]ultitudes of reverent Christians" had been able to incorporate this new knowledge into their faith, Fosdick said, "sure that all truth comes from the one God and is His revelation." This kind of change, this influx of knowledge, had happened before, Fosdick said, and whenever scientific discoveries seemed to challenge the tenets of faith, there was "only one way out—the new knowledge and the old faith had to be blended in a new combination."

But a growing number of conservative Christians were coalescing around the idea that a certain number of theological tenets were "fundamental" to the faith and therefore nonnegotiable. Between 1910 and 1915, a series of publications called *The Fundamentals* identified Christ's virgin birth, his divinity, his physical resurrection, and the inerrancy of scripture as core beliefs that could not be changed or compromised. Fosdick's argument was not that these "fundamental" beliefs themselves were necessarily wrong, but that these beliefs should not be used as some kind of litmus test—that people should not be cast out or ostracized from their faith, their churches, or from relationships with each other for holding or expressing differing beliefs. "Opinions may be mistaken," he said, "love never is."

Fosdick snuck in some zingers, charging that Jesus himself could not meet fundamentalists' strict demands. But at a time when fundamentalists had "actually endeavored to put on the statute books of a whole state binding laws against teaching modern biology," Fosdick urged Christians to incorporate scientific discoveries into their faith. For Fosdick, the future of the church depended on this kind of flexibility, humility, and openness to change: "Ministers often bewail the fact that young people turn from religion to science for the regulative ideas of their lives," Fosdick said. "But this is easily explicable. Science treats a young man's mind as though it were really important."

The impact of Fosdick's sermon, titled "Shall the Fundamentalists Win?" was seismic, as far as sermons go: John D. Rockefeller Jr. paid for 130,000 copies to be printed and mailed to every Protestant minister in the United States. Although the debate between Christian fundamentalists and more liberal Protestants did not originate with Fosdick's sermon, his clear outlining of the core issues allowed fundamentalists to hone their own message and unify their opposition in response.

William Jennings Bryan led the charge against Fosdick, arguing that he should be removed from his pulpit for his "utter agnosticism." Bryan's power and influence in conservative Christian circles had been steadily increasing as he shifted his focus from secular politics—populist causes like labor rights and the direct election of senators—to religious politics. In 1922, Bryan was one of several Christian leaders campaigning for states to introduce legislation that would ban teaching evolution in schools. He toured the country, giving lectures and writing op-eds in which he described evolution as "the greatest issue in the world." In one 1924 lecture titled, "Is the Bible True?" Bryan said, "We have a fight on our hands and I am on the defensive." But the following summer, when Bryan traveled to Dayton to make his last stand against evolution, it was as a prosecutor.

Just as Fosdick's sermon clarified the battle lines for fundamentalists, the fallout from the Scopes trial solidified in fundamentalist Christians' minds what they'd always suspected to be true: That the world was not their home; that they existed in opposition to the rising tide of secularism and liberalism. That their battle was not, and perhaps by definition would never be, over.

Inherit the Wind was itself an adaptation of a play written a few years earlier, and the film's depiction of the trial is the one most firmly cemented into the country's consciousness. Dayton's annual reenactment was originally intended to be a kind of corrective to the Hollywood interpretation: When a local playwright first suggested that Dayton host its own production of *Inherit the Wind,* a professor at Bryan College persuaded him to write a new play that adhered more closely to the trial transcripts. The new play, *Inherit the Truth,* was performed annually in Dayton for two decades.

When *Inherit the Wind* was written, in 1955, the Scopes trial was a vehicle through which to examine the then-contemporary McCarthy trials. And in the intervening decades, the Scopes trial has remained a mirror through which we try to see our own times more clearly. In the playwrights' foreword to *Inherit the Wind,* they write, "The stage directions set the time as 'Not long ago.' It might have been yesterday. It could be tomorrow."

There have been three televised performances of *Inherit the Wind,* in the 1960s, the 1980s, and the 1990s; in 2009, the BBC broadcast a radio play of the Scopes trial based on the transcripts, titled "The

Great Tennessee Monkey Trial"; the Scopes trial was even featured in a 2013 episode of Comedy Central's *Drunk History*. The Scopes trial remains evergreen for the fantasy it presents of an ultimate ideological battle, where individual people are boiled down to avatars, fully embodying two opposing positions. In the myth of the Scopes trial, one side triumphs, once and for all, over the other.

Except that it remains unclear which "side" actually won. Before the Scopes trial, Bryan had lost three presidential elections as well as his bid for moderator of his own Presbyterian denomination. But in the eyes of Christians like him, who wanted the world to reverse course, to slow its constant changing, he was a hero. And in Dayton, at perhaps the most high-profile moment of his career, he won. Not only was Scopes found guilty, but the Butler Act stayed on Tennessee's law books until 1967—more than forty years after Bryan's death.

The Sunday after the Scopes trial ended, Bryan, who was sixty-five years old, took a nap after church and died in his sleep. His death in Dayton seemed to bind him forever to this place, encasing Bryan, the Scopes trial, and Dayton together in amber. And although the story I'd always heard about the Scopes trial was that it was a moment of humiliation for fundamentalist Christians, somehow the end of something, it's clear that Bryan's death in Dayton was a new beginning, a sanctification; the town itself became a kind of holy ground.

Before Bryan's sudden death, Mencken warned that Bryan might live another ten years or more: "What he may accomplish in that time, seen here at close range, looms up immensely larger than it appears to a city man five hundred miles away." But Bryan likely accomplished even more by dying as he did, in Dayton, almost immediately after the Scopes trial ended.

When the trial ended, Darrow chose to forego making any closing remarks, which barred Bryan from delivering his own closing remarks. In the days following the trial, he arranged for their publication. Arriving as they did after his death, Bryan's closing remarks, urging Christians across the country to build Christian colleges and universities, rose to the level of divine decree. Dayton's own Bryan College was one of more than seventy Christian colleges founded across the country after the Scopes trial. Bryan College would become a leader in Christian apologetics and the formation of a Christian "worldview" for the next generation of white conservative Christians.

In the nearly one hundred years since Bryan died in Dayton, he has been eclipsed in progressive Christian circles by Dayton's most famous daughter, Rachel Held Evans, whose father is a professor of Christian Worldview Studies at Bryan College. After growing up in Dayton as a passionate evangelical Christian and attending Bryan College herself, Evans found herself unable to reconcile some of the beliefs with which she'd been raised.

In her first book, *Evolving in Monkey Town* (later retitled *Faith Unraveled*), Evans wrote about her upbringing in an evangelical faith that had been irrevocably shaped by the events of her hometown: "With the best of intentions, the generation before mine worked diligently to prepare their children to make an intelligent case for Christianity. We were constantly reminded of the superiority of our own worldview and the shortcomings of all others," she wrote. "As a result, many of us entered the world with both an unparalleled level of conviction and a crippling lack of curiosity...So prepared to defend the faith, we missed the thrill of discovering it for ourselves."

Evans eventually concluded that theology "is not the moon but rather a finger pointing at the moon." She gave up a quest for answers that would put all her questions to rest: "My hope is that if I am patient, the questions themselves will dissolve into meaning." Evans went on to publish several more books, some of them best-sellers, before she died unexpectedly of an infection in 2019, at the age of thirty-seven.

I had imagined Evans as a figure telling a new story about Dayton. But in Dayton, no one we talked to seemed to have heard of her. As we walked around downtown, my mom mentioned Evans to any person we encountered as a kind of shibboleth, but everyone responded with shrugs, blank stares, lips drawn thin.

"They know who she is, but they don't want to admit it," my mom whispered conspiratorially. "They just don't want to talk about her."

The family sitting on our aisle at the reenactment were the only people who admitted to having heard of Evans, but cautiously. They were a family of South Dakotans, recent transplants to East Tennessee who had moved here for an academic job at a nearby university. When we asked them if they had read anything by Rachel Held Evans, the man sitting next to me leaned in close and whispered, "People like her have a way of disrupting systems of power in places like this."

Aha, I thought, smugly. He was on my side.

I hear echoes of the Scopes trial everywhere, but particularly in conservative Christianity's influence on contemporary politics, in a rising tide of legislation attempting to restrict everything from public education to reproductive rights to gender expression. In 2021, Tennessee House Republicans introduced legislation that prohibits public or charter schools from teaching a long litany of topics surrounding structural racism—legislation that will likely prevent Tennessee schools from accessing new federal grants intended to help schools confront racism and inequality. A year later, new Tennessee laws limited what books could be available in school libraries; required public schools to publish a list of every book, movie, newspaper, and magazine in their libraries; and banned schools from teaching about racism and oppression under the sweeping banner of critical race theory.

Conservative Tennessee state legislators have not been able to provide any concrete examples of any Tennessee schools in which critical race theory was actually taught, but that has not stopped them from making its destruction a legislative priority. Just like John Washington Butler's account of reading stories in the paper about children turning against the Bible, legislators point to anecdotes circulated in conservative social networks about a little white girl coming home from school asking if she was racist.

After the COVID-19 pandemic forced many churches to hold worship services virtually, a Pew Research Center report compiled more than twelve thousand sermons that had been shared online during the 2020 presidential campaign and analyzed the various ways pastors of different denominations spoke about race, politics, and the pandemic. One quote, pulled from an evangelical sermon, stood out to me. "Our original sin, then, according to critical race theory, is whiteness," the pastor said. "Salvation from that fall begins when the oppressors become woke..."

Just as William Jennings Bryan justified his opposition to evolution because it challenged, for him, the idea that people were made in God's image, this pastor argued that critical race theory presents a new origin story, with a different original sin, and an altered pathway to salvation.

In a reflection on the 100th anniversary of Fosdick's sermon, the public theologian Diana Butler Bass writes that fundamentalist Christianity's response to the Scopes trial "established a pattern still present in fundamentalism: alternating between withdrawal and anger...In the last century, fundamentalists have vacillated between the two responses by either casting themselves as unprotected victims in retreat from a cruel world out to get them or projecting their ideas of sin and judgment onto the larger body politic with vengeance."

In "Shall the Fundamentalists Win?" Fosdick concluded that fundamentalists would not win the heart of Christianity: "I do not believe for one moment that the Fundamentalists are going to succeed," he said. But with the distance a full century provides, it's hard to feel so sure. The hundredth anniversary of Fosdick's sermon fell on the summer of 2022, when a string of Supreme Court cases involving abortion, prayer in public schools, and gun ownership were seen as triumphs for conservative evangelicals.

A century after Fosdick predicted that fundamentalists would not win, fundamentalist theological influence on politics is rising—with a devastating toll on people's lives. After the Supreme Court overturned *Roe v. Wade*, Tennessee's trigger ban went into immediate effect, banning all abortions with extremely limited exceptions. In the summer of 2023, Murfreesboro briefly made homosexuality illegal as part of a sweeping ban on "public indecency."

In February of 2024, the state's Republican governor, Bill Lee—who is a member of what's been called an "uber evangelical" church—signed a bill protecting clergy members who refused to perform wedding ceremonies for same-sex couples. He also proposed a statewide voucher program for private schools. One investigation showed that 84 percent of the schools approved for this program were private religious schools, most of them Christian. Later that spring, Lee signed bills into law making November "Christian Heritage Month" and designating the Aitkin Bible one of Tennessee's official state books.

These recent examples from my home state are part of a larger movement as restrictive legislation, shaped by conservative Christian ideology, continues to sweep the South—and elsewhere in the U.S. where conservative evangelicalism has a foothold in politics. In February of 2024, the Alabama Supreme Court offered up one of the most damning and confounding rulings by granting personhood to embryos, effectively shutting down IVF treatments across the state—and paving the way for other states to do the same. In his concurring opinion, Tom Parker, the chief justice of the Alabama Supreme Court, cited theology as the basis for his legal decision, writing, "Human life cannot be wrongfully destroyed without incurring the wrath of a holy God, who views the destruction of His image as an affront to Himself."

That same month, a nonbinary high school student in Owasso, Oklahoma, named Nex Benedict died after being attacked by fellow students in a public school bathroom. Benedict's death came less than two years after Ryan Walters, an anti-trans politician who advocated for Christianity in public schools, became the Oklahoma State Superintendent of Public Instruction as that state experienced its own rounds of conservative legislation restricting gender-affirming care and access to books in schools.

In the weeks after Benedict's death, the *Washington Post* published its findings that hate crimes targeting LBGTQ people had risen sharply in recent years, more than quadrupling in states where legislation restricted the rights and education of LBGTQ students. Walters was unrepentant. In an interview with the *New York Times* shortly after Benedict's death, Walters said, "There's not multiple genders. There's two. That's how God created us."

Perhaps the fundamentalist beliefs often driving these waves of legislation can be justified by certain interpretations of scripture, but it's hard to believe this perspective on the world has been shaped more by faith than by the worldlier forces of power and politics. Conservative evangelicalism may be less a theological movement, at its core, than a cultural and political one. As conservative Christian politicians, church leaders, and lay people alike rally around legislation stripping women of their bodily autonomy and reproductive rights; outlawing gender-affirming healthcare and criminalizing gender-nonconforming behavior like drag performances; all the while narrowing what perspectives on American history are allowed to be taught in schools that they're actively defunding, what they're really doing is enforcing a kind of civic fundamentalism, attacking anything that falls outside of its rigid binaries and hierarchies.

It has always seemed weird to me that Christianity is even susceptible to this kind of binary thinking. Christ's followers ostensibly model their lives and values after a man who was both human and divine; who was both dead and resurrected; who appeared, after death, to eat fish with his friends, ascended into heaven, and yet also remains alive, in spirit, for his followers two thousand years later (not to mention a man who *explicitly* associated his own arrival on earth with the end of binaries and hierarchies: in Galatians 3:28, Jesus said, "There is no longer Jew or Gentile, slave or free, male and female. For you are all one in Christ Jesus.").

Many queer, trans, and nonbinary people of faith remind us that scripture does not and cannot contain the whole world. M Barclay, a nonbinary United Methodist deacon, writes that the creation story "talks about night and day and land and water, but we have dusk and we have marshes. These verses don't mean 'there's only land and water, and there's nowhere where these two meet.' These binaries aren't meant to speak to all of reality—they invite us into thinking about everything between and beyond."

Reading this, I thought about my coworker and friend, Nathan, a seminarian who left his conservative Southern Baptist upbringing behind when he came out. He'd landed in the United Methodist Church, just in time to see its slow, painful split over the full inclusion of LGBTQ members. Nathan and I had recently gone on an absurd road trip for work, driving four hours to a fundraising luncheon and four hours back, on his birthday, in the pouring rain. We talked, as usual, about faith and theology, and I wrote down something he said that day and thought about it often: "These texts don't have any inherent meaning outside of the meaning that we as a community decide to give them."

This sentence, shrugged off by Nathan as he drove, has stayed with me, returning to my mind often. I had never consciously thought of scriptural interpretation as a decision made within the context of community, as a prism through which we could discern a community's choices about what—or who—was important to them. No matter whether you believe the Bible is the literal word of God, handed down from on high, or a collection of texts formed and revised over centuries, the Bible doesn't tell you how to read it, what meaning to take from it. It is too contradictory, too fickle, too strange to pretend otherwise. Any interpretation is a choice that says far more about the person or community doing the interpreting than it does about the text itself.

There is no single descriptive name that can encapsulate all the changes happening within the Christian right in America. For years I've thought about evangelicals and fundamentalists like squares and rectangles: Not all evangelicals are fundamentalists, while all fundamentalists were, fundamentally, evangelical. Fosdick himself had a similar equation: "All Fundamentalists are conservatives," he said, while "not all conservatives are Fundamentalists." Writing in the *New York Times* in 2024, columnist David French described American evangelicalism as "a combination of three religious traditions: fundamentalism, evangelicalism and Pentecostalism."

I've seen an increasing effort to make these distinctions more precise, highlighting branches of conservative Christianity like Dominionism, Christian Nationalism, the Seven Mountain Mandate, and the New Apostolic Reformation's insistence on spiritual warfare. Rev. David Gushee, a post-evangelical Christian ethicist, uses the term "Authoritarian Reactionary Christianity" which speaks helpfully to the way this kind of Christianity moves in—and against—the world.

As a shorthand, however imperfect, fundamentalism describes the mindset shared by many of these Christians, no matter how they would, as individuals, identify more specifically. But lately it can feel difficult to find much daylight between any of these distinctions, and even harder to locate fundamentalism as a strictly religious phenomenon.

Membership in mainline Protestant denominations began to decline sharply in the 1960s and '70s. For a while, the shrinking of mainline Protestant churches seemed only to benefit evangelical and nondenominational churches, whose numbers swelled into the early 2000s. Lately, membership in evangelical and nondenominational churches have been in decline, too, following overall trends in American Christianity.

I had hoped that the problem of Christian fundamentalism might be answered as Americans continue leaving the church in droves; as the percentage of Americans claiming any kind of Christian faith declines. Perhaps my personal data set skews my expectations: Every year, my friend group expands to include more millennial "exvangelicals" engaged in the process of deconstructing the conservative faith traditions that formed them. Most of them, rather than trying to reconstruct a new version of their faith, end up leaving the church behind, for good.

This particular portion of the decline in American Christianity comes not, as fundamentalists would like to believe, from the outside—from a secular, mainstream society's corrupting influence —but from within. The writer Danté Stewart argues that the greatest threat to Christianity is not secularism, but certainty: "When you are so convinced that you are right, then you will create all types of enemies and cut yourself off from the ways God is active in another person's experience."

The former believers I've come to know have found that in attempting to create a sealed, static relationship with sacred texts and with God, fundamentalism creates a deeply unsatisfying theology that is at odds not only with complex human relationships in a constantly changing world, but with scripture itself: As Fosdick said, "in the Bible these elements are not final…they are always being superseded; revelation is progressive."

But a decline in church membership and attendance doesn't necessarily equal a decline in influence or power or even a change in beliefs. When the evangelical publication *Christianity Today* studied what happened when white Southern evangelicals left the church, they found that these former churchgoers "don't lose the church's political conservatism, moralism, or individualism. Instead, they become hyper-individualistic, strongly devoted to law and order, and overwhelmingly politically conservative."

As she researched and wrote her book *Jesus and John Wayne: How White Evangelicals Corrupted a Faith and Fractured a Nation,* American historian Kristin Kobes Du Mez discovered "striking levels of theological illiteracy among evangelicals." What defined an evangelical, she found, was "participation in an evangelical culture of consumption," rather than beliefs, worship practices, or faith traditions. "Did you grow up listening to 'Focus on the Family' in your home each and every day? Did you shop at Christian bookstores? Did you listen to Christian music or Christian talk radio?" For evangelicals, she says, orthodoxy is defined not theologically, but socially and politically.

Reading Du Mez, I think of the symbols of white Christian nationalism on display during the January 6, 2021 insurrection: the crosses, the white Jesuses, the Bible verses on clothing and flags. In his testimony to a House Select Committee, a D.C. Metropolitan Police Officer testified, "It was clear the terrorists perceived themselves to be Christians." When a religion becomes inseparable from political ideology, these symbols seem to depart from their previous associations and live out a kind of secular fundamentalism.

Shortly after January 6, 2021, the editors of *Religion & Politics* wrote a series of responses to the attempted insurrection. Lerone A. Martin, an Associate Professor of Religion and Politics and a self-professed born-again believer raised in the evangelical church, warned of the dangers of "a white nationalist political party masquerading as a church." He ended his letter by asking, "What does it profit a body of believers to gain political appointments and lose its own soul?"

So what to do about fundamentalism? Mencken argued that fundamentalists should be mocked and shamed, laughed out of town. He finished his coverage of the Scopes trial with an article written just hours after Bryan died, in which Mencken wallowed in meanness, relishing every cruel syllable: "Bryan was a vulgar and common man, a cad undiluted," he wrote. "He was ignorant, bigoted, self-seeking, blatant, and dishonest. His career brought him into contact with the first men of his time; he preferred the company of rustic ignoramuses...He was a peasant come home to the dung-pile."

Confronted with fundamentalists' absolutism, perhaps an equal-and-opposite absolutism, like Mencken's, feels like the necessary response. Lately it seems like any person, holding any "worldview," is susceptible to a certain kind of fundamentalism, an uncompromising attachment to their own position. So fundamentalism shifts, from a theological perspective to a psychological one. Perhaps that is how fundamentalism wins, in the end: not by one "side" winning over another, but by fundamentalism itself spreading as it divides the world into neatly delineated, distinct "sides" with no overlapping areas of shared values, perspectives, or concern.

Shortly after the reenactment, when I looked up the complete court transcripts of the Scopes trial, I found myself drawn to the bracketed notes marking any audible interruption: *[Laughter.] [Applause.] [A train whistle blows.]* I found it so comforting to imagine the audience's unruly reaction, or a train's whistle so loud that all the arguments had to fall silent until it passed: All these reminders of a world continuing on outside the four walls of the courtroom. These outbursts, memorialized in the black and white text of the transcripts, are a reminder: For all our attempts to create an airtight worldview, the world itself breaks through.

The morning after the reenactment, my parents and I checked out of our motel rooms. Outside, the only signs of life were a group of migrant farm workers, traveling in four dusty school buses, shouting as they cannon-balled into the motel pool. We stopped at a coffee shop named, of course, for Bryan, and got breakfast. The strip mall along the highway seemed semi-abandoned, surrounded by a bleak expanse of pavement and empty storefronts. Mid-morning, my parents traveled east, toward a vacation in the mountains. I headed west, back home, on wide, empty highways threaded between gentle hills.

Though I had envisioned Dayton as a kind of outlier—a specific place where a specific story was retold over and over again, it seems to me now that if Dayton is unique in any way, it is only because it is so explicit in its refusal to leave the past behind, in its desire to relive it, year after year. In her book *South to America: A Journey Below the Mason-Dixon to Understand the Soul of a Nation,* Imani Perry writes that we live in the past "as a changing same. The only possibility is reinterpretation of the scriptural underpinnings."

And it is reinterpretation I keep coming back to. If, in a place like Dayton, history were reinterpreted, rather than simply reenacted, how might that open up possibilities for new insights, revelations, and wisdom for our own time? It seems that whenever history, or scripture, or even beliefs cannot be reinterpreted, they cease to be living, instructive, or meaningful to our lives. They become, instead, the empty scaffolding of a worldview.

By being linked so irrevocably to the creation story found in Genesis, evolution now seems imbued with its own "scriptural underpinnings" and theological implications. As a new story—even as an alternate origin story—evolution suggests to me that we are not the finished product. Instead, we are the promise of ongoing change that will extend far beyond any of our individual lives. We have been otherwise before, and if we continue on this earth long enough, we will be otherwise again. Thanks be to God.

On the highway driving west, I passed billboards claiming to speak for God; on the radio, on one station after another, men's voices did the same. They all sounded so sure. I turned the radio off and drove in silence. Before I ever knew about Fosdick or his most famous sermon, I grew up singing one of his hymns, often, in church, and I found myself humming it as I began the long drive home:

From the fears that long have bound us
Free our hearts to faith and praise
Grant us wisdom, grant us courage
For the living of these days
For the living of these days.

NATURAL ENDS

ALONG THE WINDING ROAD clinging to the edge of the Ocoee River, dozens of makeshift memorials marked each tight turn. I drove past hillsides streaked with a thin dusting of snow, crossing from Tennessee to Georgia, back to Tennessee, briefly to North Carolina, and back to South Carolina, twisting through porous state lines every few miles. Rumpled mountains slid through the rearview window, and the road unfurled, straightening for a moment, as I passed a church sign reading HEAVEN IS JUST A BREATH AWAY.

I lost an hour overnight to daylight savings, another on the road to the eastern time zone, and a third to standstill traffic outside of Chattanooga. This trip, my first time traveling alone since my son was born, arrived when I was three weeks into an unending cold, brought home from my son's daycare. But I wasn't flustered by these delays and inconveniences the way I would have been before having a child. A year and a half into motherhood, most days have been a struggle against this kind of loss, against hours slipping away almost unnoticed.

The plan was to spend a week visiting conservation cemeteries across the South, starting with Ramsey Creek Preserve, the nation's first conservation burial ground, which Dr. Billy and Kimberley Campbell opened in rural South Carolina in 1998. At Ramsey Creek, bodies are buried in a biodegradable container like a shroud or a pine box, and without the chemical embalming and vault that have become common—and sometimes required—in conventional cemeteries. The revenue generated by burials funds the preservation and restoration of the seventy-eight-acre preserve.

In the Ramsey Creek parking lot, there are printed maps showing the preserve's hiking trails. I was looking over the maps, blowing my nose into a bandana, when Kimberley met me. She was friendly and outgoing, wearing pink and purple leggings printed with galaxies and stars. As we walked, she stopped every few feet to expound encyclopedically on a wide range of topics: Ethiopian church forests, or a degenerative disease that women from an indigenous tribe in Papua New Guinea contracted from eating the brains of their deceased relatives, or the questions she got most often from people who lived nearby: "Won't animals dig me up?" she recited. "Won't the bodies poison the water?"

Kimberley laughed, but then listed with some exasperation the real threats to the water: erosion, chicken farms, unregulated manure. As for any dangers posed by decomposing bodies, she said, embalming fluids—which are outlawed in places like Ramsey Creek—are the real contaminants. Then she turned to me where I stood coughing into my mask. "To be frank," she said, "you're a lot more contagious right now than you would be if you were dead."

We walked a worn footpath leading to a small, century-old white chapel that Kimberley and Billy had moved, on a flatbed truck, from its previous location and restored. Ramsey Creek visitors hold funerals here, or weddings, or family reunions. Mounds of earth surrounded the chapel in haphazard formations. Some, with scattered rose petals clinging to the dry grass, seemed like more recent burials, while others had already begun receding into the earth. The effect was strange. It's not unusual, of course, to see a churchyard full of graves, but the earthen mounds conjured a human body—a human life—more immediately and intimately than any headstone I've ever seen.

Inside the chapel, the stained-glass windows depicted lady slipper orchids, southern nodding trillium, and dragonflies alongside extinct species like Carolina parakeets and passenger pigeons. The windows brought together the species—living and extinct—that would have once made a home here on this land Billy and Kimberley have devoted their lives to protecting.

The forested trail Kimberley and I walked was lined on either side by mounded graves, some of them marked by flat stones engraved with names and dates. I noted the names as we passed: Ann, Joyce, Russell, Patricia. When I asked Kimberley if many of the people buried here lived nearby, she said that people come from all over. She gestured to the graves, reciting where each person had come from: one from Florida, another from Maryland; a man whose body was flown from California; a woman whose body had been driven down from Memphis in the back of her son's Suburban.

If it seems that flying a body from the other side of the country, or driving a body from another state, might defeat the purpose of a place like Ramsey Creek, the solution, to Kimberley, is not to be cremated or to be buried in a conventional cemetery closer to home. The solution is even more conservation cemeteries, scattered across the country, so that no one is too far from a final resting place like Ramsey Creek.

The environmental costs of conventional burial in a park-style cemetery, with their green lawns maintained through mowing, watering, and pesticide use, are well-documented. The Green Burial Council estimates that conventional U.S. cemeteries leach more than 4 million gallons of embalming fluid into the ground each year, not to mention the 64,000 tons of steel and 1.6 million tons of concrete used in caskets and vaults. And while cremation is less environmentally hazardous than conventional burial, it is not without costs of its own: A single cremation requires heating an oven to over 2,000 degrees for two hours, and releases roughly the same emissions as driving a car 500 miles. For many people considering the environmental ethics of death care, cremation might seem like simply the least bad option.

More than half of the dead in the U.S. are cremated each year, and the National Funeral Directors Association predicts that by 2040 the U.S. cremation rate will reach 78.4 percent. But cremation rates continue to lag across the South. This might be because religious custom often favors conventional burial; various branches of Christianity have historically had an uneasy relationship with cremation, which troubles, for some, the notion of bodily resurrection.

After Ramsey Creek Preserve opened in 1998, Billy drafted the standards for conservation cemeteries which would be adopted by the Green Burial Council, which was founded in 2005 to provide certification standards for green burial practices. Since the opening of Ramsey Creek Preserve, conservation cemeteries have popped up across the United States. The success of conservation cemeteries across the South is due in large part to the influence of the Campbells themselves, who opened Ramsey Creek with the goal of preserving one million acres of land through an ever-expanding network of conservation cemeteries, and who now spend much of their time working as consultants to people who want to open conservation cemeteries of their own. On a quick phone call with me one morning, Kimberley off-handedly listed eighteen conservation cemeteries they'd helped get started. Since Ramsey Creek opened, conservation cemeteries have popped up across South Carolina, Georgia, Florida, Tennessee, Virginia, and North Carolina.

I've asked Billy Campbell why he thinks the South has been receptive to natural burial. Billy, who is a medical doctor in Westminster,

South Carolina, and also runs a home hospice care company, told me that many Southerners are only a generation or two removed from traditional death care practices. Billy's own grandparents told him stories about sitting up with the bodies of loved ones overnight and digging graves by hand. Many graveyards were run by churches, and congregations were familiar with caring for their own dead. There is a "latent connection," Billy says, between Southerners and death care, that still lingers here.

In *Greening Death,* Suzanne Kelly compares caring for the dead—an act that was once carried out mostly at home, and mostly by women—to childbirth. When childbirth was medicalized—and when death care was privatized and monetized—what was lost was not simply a consumer choice, as it is often described, but a foundational wisdom.

This connection between birth and death made immediate sense to me. I'd started thinking about death all the time after my son's birth, when I returned from the hospital cut open, with a baby I could only hold on a pillow balanced on my lap. After my infected incision was reopened, I spent my first postpartum months hooked up to IV antibiotics, wearing a wound vac, bewildered by sudden frailty and fear. Giving birth made death apparent, made an immediate reality of something that once seemed theoretical and far-off.

I found none of this foundational wisdom in the care my son and I received during and after his birth. And it is this kind of wisdom that is ultimately at stake in conversations about death care: "The potential of such an earth-bound ethic of human death won't be found in its capacity to offer environmentally sustainable end-of-life options," Kelly writes. "Its greatest promise lies in stimulating a change in the way people see themselves in terms of being a part of, and not apart from, nature."

As we hiked past a rushing stream, I asked Kimberley about the latest technological innovations in death care, from infinity suits to human composting. She dismissed them all as "hokey." She said that the millions of dollars that have been funneled into new industries like Recompose, the human composting company based in Washington state, should have been used to preserve and protect land from development. "*The land* is the composting machine," she said. "*The land* is the infinity suit."

For Billy and Kimberley, everything comes back to protecting land. They got into natural burial pragmatically, as a way to fund land conservation and restoration. But their decades working in natural burial have made them passionate about death care, too. Billy often tells the story of the first person they buried at Ramsey Creek, a friend's stillborn baby. "When you bury the first body it changes the feel of the land," Billy wrote on the Ramsey Creek website.

When they first opened Ramsey Creek, Billy expected a certain kind of customer: "I thought we'd rely more on people from Greenville, Atlanta—the cities. People who are environmentalists. People like me. But it's turned out that a big part of our clientele are people of faith. Assemblies of God. Evangelicals."

We were walking up a steep hill when Kimberley stopped abruptly and turned to face me, as she had many times that morning, and told me a story about a woman who had visited from Augusta, Georgia. "We were just talking and walking around," Kimberley said. "Finally, the woman said, 'You know how important my church is to me. I've been going there for forty years. But the church was an edifice built by men to worship God.'" The woman looked around, held up her hands. The wind rustled the trees, bathing her and Kimberley in dappled light. "This *is* God."

Many of the people I've spoken with have an evangelical zeal for natural burial. One woman, a pastor who attended the seminary where I worked, told me about her plans: "When I die, I've instructed my family to wrap me in one of my quilts and put me in the ground," she said. "To do anything other than that, I believe, goes against God's plan from the beginning."

What she's referring to by "the beginning" is a verse found in the book of Genesis that I heard countless times as I traveled through the South speaking to people involved in natural burial: "By the sweat of your brow you will eat your food until you return to the ground, since from it you were taken; for dust you are and to dust you will return." These are the final lines of what is often interpreted as God's curse on Adam and Eve for eating the forbidden fruit: Not only are they exiled from the Garden of Eden and doomed to toil and pain throughout their lives, they are doomed, finally, to die, and to return to the dust from which God made them. In Genesis, death—and the body's return to the dust from which it came—is often interpreted as a punishment for original sin. But in this way, it has always seemed, to me, like a kind of reconciliation—a return to the world from which we've been exiled.

For many conservative Christians, natural burial is appealing because, as one funeral director told me, it's "what the Bible says we're supposed to do." Getting rid of embalming and caskets and vaults, the body is allowed to enter into the world's cycles of decay—returning to dust—more directly.

In July 2021, Pastor Matt Williams, one of the head pastors of South Carolina's nondenominational Grace Church, with more than ten locations in and around Greenville, South Carolina, announced that the church had purchased twelve acres of land to be used as a cemetery where they could bury their own members without embalming or a vault. Williams gave four reasons for this new venture. The first was the environment. "We are putting toxins in the ground," Williams said. "We're called to be good stewards of the world that God's given us. We don't know how much longer this world's gonna last but it's our job to take care of it."

The second reason was economics: If 5,000 members of Grace Church each spent $7,500 on a funeral, "that's 37.5 million dollars that we are going to put in the ground in the next 50 years." But if Grace Church members were able to lower those funeral costs to $2,000, with that money going back into the church via burial at the church's own cemetery, Williams asked, "What can we do with all the money we save?"

The third reason Williams gave was hope in the resurrection. Embalming, he argued, offered a false hope that the body would be preserved from decay. This desire for preservation through embalming "misdirects us from the God that created me," Williams said. "I am completely dependent [on] and hope in Him to recreate me."

The fourth and final reason for the Grace Church cemetery was community: Williams envisioned teams of church members building boxes and making shrouds; a team organizing the burial and funeral; a team managing the land and digging the graves. "This"—he said, meaning death—"is the future for all of us. Jesus could come back tomorrow, but every generation thinks that. So we want to be anticipating him and also preparing."

Religious language has a way of creeping into conversations about climate change and environmentalism. There are discussions of "belief" and "doubt"; environmental advocates agonize over how to "convert" people who are skeptical of climate change—especially white evangelical Christians—to "believers" who will put their faith and collective influence into action to curb the worst effects of a warming climate. As I left Ramsey Creek and drove an hour east to Grace Church's new cemetery, I wondered if burial—a rite of passage in which the material, physical world and any spiritual sense of a life beyond it are always inherently entwined—could offer an entry point for conservative Christians who might otherwise feel uneasy with climate change activism or environmentalism.

In his sermon, Pastor Williams was careful to clarify that the church was not going green. "Green Burial," Williams said, was "not really a Christian thing. It was mostly environmentalists." When I spoke with Pastor Matt Kelley, a church elder who's taken the lead on the cemetery project, he told me that they were not concerned with meeting any requirements set by organizations like the Green Burial Council. "We're just representing dust to dust," he said.

Driving from the foothills to the piedmont of South Carolina, the road unspooled like a thread. As the land flattened, I passed several small churches, all Baptist, all with attached graveyards. I missed it at first—the unmarked gravel road that leads to Grace Church's new cemetery. I turned around, parked my car in a cloud of red dust, and met Matt Kelley beside his truck.

Matt seemed very uneasy about talking with me. Over email, I tried to reassure him: I was a preacher's kid; I grew up in the church; I worked at a seminary. Finally, he agreed to a phone conversation, with two other church staff members, both women—who Matt referred to as "the girls"—present on the call.

"The thing is," Matt said, "it's not so much about the land but the process of what we do for our people with burial—and what we're saying we're *not* going to do: no embalming, no vault. We dig the hole. Our people lower the body and bury the body. It's turned out to be very, very good for our people. We've buried four so far."

The Grace Church cemetery was a flat, sunbaked rectangle with a massive set of power lines running down the middle. There was no signage, no indication that this place was owned by a church or used for burial. When Grace Church bought the land, it was covered in eight-foot-tall holly trees which church members have been digging up and replanting around the edges in order to provide some structure. Where Ramsey Creek could have been mistaken for a state park, with its clearly marked hiking trails, forested hills, and clear, rushing streams, the Grace Church cemetery looked like no place in particular. This spoke to the malleable nature of natural burial, which can be adapted to fit the land or community it serves. But it also seemed to illuminate how natural cemeteries can be an expression of those communities and what they value: while Ramsey Creek was an expression of its founders' commitment to conservation, the Grace Church cemetery spoke most of all to expediency, to meeting a need as it expressed itself.

Jennifer Dill, the church's natural burial coordinator, met us at the back of the property, where she showed me a neat row of four slightly mounded graves covered in crisp brown pine needles. Two of the graves had small stones lying flat on the ground, while the other two were, so far, unmarked. Jennifer was slight, and kept her short hair tucked into a tiny ponytail. She described the church as historically being with their members "from cradle to death" before the funeral home stepped in. "But we want to be cradle to grave."

When they got the call for their first burial, earlier than they expected, Jennifer grabbed a nightstand from her house and improvised a graveside ceremony. In the hours before their first burial, they practiced carrying Matt from the hearse to the grave, lowering Matt into the ground. When the time came for the burial, "the Lord provided," Jennifer said.

Every time I spoke with Grace Church leaders, I noticed how often they used the phrase "our people." When Matt told me there had been "mixed reviews" from church members in the initial months, he said, "The complaint we hear the most from our people is that we are disrupting the culture. But the form of burial they're used to is only a hundred years old. We as a church want to be in the middle of this with our people."

Jennifer added, "We are walking our people home."

This phrase—"our people"—was repeated so consistently in my conversations with Grace Church leaders that I started to make note each time I heard it, as I had the growing realization that everything I'd told them about myself in order to develop some comfort with me and my prying questions likely had the opposite effect. Growing up in the mainline Protestant church, working at an ecumenical seminary, never explicitly calling myself a Christian—all these identifiers I'd offered likely revealed that I was not, in fact, their people.

When we first talked, Matt had just one question for me: "Do you go to church?" A flush of heat rose to my cheeks. I told them that all I'd ever known were my father's churches, and that my father had recently retired from the ministry, and after he retired I'd intended to find out what I actually would want in a faith community of my own. But then I got pregnant, and the pandemic hit, and now I had a toddler. I was quiet for a minute.

"On Christmas Eve, I took my son to church for the first time," I told them. "At a church down the street from our house. And I cried the whole time. Through every song, every prayer."

I felt my voice catch then, remembering standing in the pews, the feeling of my son's weight in my arms as I tried to sing through sudden tears and my dampened mask. When my son got fidgety, we roamed the church basement, playing hide and seek in the empty Sunday School classrooms, hiding in the choir robes, wandering these spaces that had made up the geography of my entire world, growing up.

I didn't tell him about the day, shortly before that Christmas Eve service, when I stepped into my father's backyard and found him sitting by the fire pit, in a blue cloud of smoke, burning stacks of his handwritten sermons indiscriminately.

"Anyway," I said, aware of silence on the other end of the phone. "I'm sure there's some unresolved stuff there." I wasn't sure where this story had even come from, why I'd brought it up, why I had to work to keep from crying as I told it. I wasn't sure why I couldn't just answer his question with a simple "no."

Circling back to our cars, we stood under the power lines with their faint electric hum. The heat had climbed over the last hour. Matt's forehead gleamed with pinpricks of sweat.

"I'm pretty nervous about this," Matt said. "I've read your work. You write about your dad."

He said it sort of like a question, but didn't elaborate. I nodded, and we stood there in heavy silence. I wasn't sure what he was implying, or wondering. It was not the first time I'd felt that way. Even natural burial—what we, ostensibly, have in common—seemed to mean entirely different things to us.

It seemed to me that, in addition to responding to our disconnection from our bodies' own death and decay, conservation cemeteries have the potential to heal some of the damaging beliefs people hold about our relationship with the natural world—many of which come from those lines in Genesis, in which not only death, but also estrangement from God and from nature, are often interpreted as punishment for original sin. This interpretation can lead to a kind of Calvinist relationship with the natural world, in which humans, in their state of total depravity, are essentially fallen, and so the only impacts people can have on nature are necessarily negative.

A similar argument has been made by environmentalists in support of cremation, who—with slogans like "Save the Land for the Living"—have tended to focus on land scarcity and land use. "But rhetoric over land loss did nothing to create a culture of belonging to it," Suzanne Kelly writes. "That language has just been another vehicle for distance and denial from death where the more-than-human continues to find belonging to the elements but where the human's best gift to the environment is only to be found in transcendence from it."

This is the environmental and spiritual influence behind the idealized image of pristine wilderness, sealed off and protected from the damaging influence of humans. Conservation cemeteries, it seemed to me, managed to counter this view, protecting and restoring vast acreage not by removing humans from the land, but by literally embedding their bodies within it.

But Matt emphasized that they discouraged church members from seeing the cemetery as a place they could go to be present with deceased loved ones. He told me people's attachment to visiting the graves of their loved ones could be a form of idolatry. "If you're a Christian," he said, "this is not your final resting place. You're with the Lord."

As I drove away from the cemetery, waving at Matt and Jennifer as they locked the gate across the driveway, I couldn't stop thinking about something Matt said when we talked on the phone, a phrase I'd written down and underlined: "This world is not your home," he'd said, his voice bright and confident. "And we are going to push that in your face."

What I saw, in natural burial, as a movement toward this world, was translated through the theology I encountered at Grace Church as a move away from it. At the Grace Church cemetery, new practices bringing the body and the earth closer together collided with long-standing beliefs that Christians are "not of this world." But perhaps the boundaries between these actions and beliefs that seemed so at odds with each other were more permeable, more slippery, than they seemed.

At the hotel that night, I watched videos of Pastor Williams preaching on the Grace Church website. "You're gonna have to have a physical body for a physical world," he said, recounting that when Jesus was resurrected, he returned to earth still marked by the scars of his crucifixion. As he talked, my hand went automatically to the uneven c-section scar stretched taut across my belly. "There is some continuity between this world and the next world," Pastor Williams said, looking momentarily flustered. "That's what I'd like to say to you. And I'd love to try to make it make sense."

In the morning, I left South Carolina and drove four hours to the hills of East Tennessee. As I drove, I thought about a funeral I had attended in Kentucky, years earlier, for a man who had died while running a quick errand, while his wife took a nap at home. The pastor pointed at the casket next to him and said repeatedly, "That's not Sam. That's just a shell."

I looked at Sam's grieving family on the front row, still reeling after his sudden, unexpected death. I don't know how I would've felt in their situation. I didn't know how it felt to hear the body of their loved one described as a shell. But I was tempted to try and imagine what it would be like for their pastor to honor the body of their lost husband, father, grandfather, and friend—to affirm that the body in the casket before them was in fact a body they had known and loved for many years—years that were still, somehow, not enough. In that moment, to deny that the body lying before them was, in fact, the person they loved, seemed a kind of violence.

This denial of Sam's body seemed related to the evangelical denial of this world as the real world. In one of Pastor Williams's recorded sermons, which I'd found on the Grace Church website and had listened to a few weeks before this trip, he said, "We are living in a shadow world. We've taught ourselves to think this is the real world, but it's really the shadow world of the world to come."

Lost in the winding back roads north of Knoxville, I tried to turn left where a man in a truck covered in extra-large IMPEACH BIDEN bumper stickers was parked to check his mail. He informed me that the road Google Maps was instructing me to drive down was not a road at all, but his driveway. He gave me instructions—turn right on Tater Valley Road, then follow the creek until the left-hand turn at the hand-painted sign. I asked him if he was sure there wasn't an ecological literacy center at the end of his driveway. He laughed, told me not to trust Google for everything, and waved me on.

It was gorgeous, early spring-green, everything damp and just-emerging. I passed a horse, close enough to touch from my car, drinking from a clear, rushing creek, and turned into the Narrow Ridge Earth Literacy Center parking lot. A woman with cropped curly gray hair, wearing overalls and a flannel shirt, was sitting on the ground, waiting for me. She told me her name was Beth, and that she had been deputized to show me around while Mitzi Wood-Von Mizener, the director of Narrow Ridge, and Bill Nickle, the founder, were out on a hike.

Beth and I drove up the gravel road, along a hillside studded with mounded graves, many of them blanketed by dried wild grasses and wildflowers, layers of straw and red soil, some daffodils wilting after last week's snow. We parked on this windbeaten hillside deep in the weathered mountains, encircled by rolling hills. Off to the side there was a backhoe parked next to a solar-powered bathroom with a composting toilet. On the burial ground, there was a timber frame structure they use for funeral services, with a bell fashioned out of an old oxygen tank swaying in the breeze. We stood there for a while, looking around, listening to the sound of crows calling to each other, and then Beth left me to it.

Anybody who agrees to the terms of their burial agreement is allowed to bury anybody at Narrow Ridge, on a donation basis with no charge to folks facing financial difficulties. Family and friends can dig the graves themselves, or for a few hundred bucks a local backhoe operator will dig for them. Narrow Ridge has buried not only people who valued natural burial and environmental sustainability, but those whose families simply couldn't afford any other option.

This financial aspect of Narrow Ridge spoke to some of environmentalism's troubling economic entanglements. While capitalism and wealth inequality often make sustainability into a series of virtuous choices available to people with financial resources, Narrow Ridge is a reminder that burial doesn't have to cost anything at all. Nowhere else did the financial burden of a conventional burial seem so evidently absurd. And while natural burial is often marketed as a more environmentally and financially sustainable option for a conscientious consumer, the vibe at Narrow Ridge was more essential:

You're going to die and leave a body behind, the hillsides around me seemed to say. *Might as well do it here. We've got space.*

Narrow Ridge requires all grave markers to be made of native stone and flush to the ground. The cemetery at Narrow Ridge doesn't appear to have a grid or firm borders—the mounds have been planted with native grasses and flowers, and as they spread they blend into one another, running counter to the conventional cemetery's insistence on each person occupying a distinct, individual bit of square footage for eternity. At Narrow Ridge, there were no such distinctions or demarcations. When it's time to move on to the next hillside designated as a burial ground, this patch of ground will be left to grow. The trees will rise, the grasses and flowers will spread, the mounds will recede into the ground. It will look like any other place.

By the time Mitzi introduced me to Bill, saying "Here's the miracle worker," I was anxious to talk to him. Bill founded Narrow Ridge half a century ago on forty acres of land with the dream of offering wilderness experiences for young adults. Back then he was a local pastor serving a four-point charge—United Methodist lingo for four congregations at once. Today, Narrow Ridge Earth Literacy Center has expanded to encompass over 500 acres of land. They offer year-round environmental sustainability programming and immersive retreats, and several families live there full-time, on parcels of land leased from Narrow Ridge in accordance with a land trust model. Most of the homes are off-grid, with features like passive solar design, strawbale construction, and rainwater collection.

The questions I'd prepared slipped away, and all I wanted was to ask him about his journey from United Methodist pastor to local sustainability guru. Does the version of himself that was a pastor still surface in his daily life now? Maybe what I want to know is how one moves between selves. I'd wanted to talk to him about the ways I was beginning to understand my father's departure from the church that once defined us both, about the day I stepped into the backyard to find him sitting by the firepit, tossing his sermons into the flames. But Bill, though warm and personable, became inscrutable whenever I tried to steer the conversation back to his long career as a pastor and his journey to Narrow Ridge.

I'd thought Narrow Ridge might be a kind of happy middle between the environmentally-motivated Ramsey Creek and the religiously-motivated Grace Church, the blend of ecological and spiritual that I thought might clarify everything for me. But perhaps I was missing the point. Bill chose the name Narrow Ridge after reading correspondence between the Jewish theologian Martin Buber and his biographer: "I have occasionally described my standpoint to my friends as the narrow ridge," Buber wrote. "I wanted by this to express that I did not rest on the broad upland of a system that includes a series of sure statements about the absolute, but on a narrow rocky ridge between the gulfs where there is no sureness of expressible knowledge." Buber's biographer would elaborate that the narrow ridge "is no 'happy middle,'" but rather the "paradoxical unity" of what one might typically see as opposites.

It was getting cold out, the sun dimming as it slipped behind the mountains. It was clear to me that I had taken too many cold meds; my brain felt six inches away from my skull; I couldn't quite access my thoughts. After talking for half an hour, I told them I was going back to Knoxville to check into a hotel. I didn't have cell service, so Bill told me he would lead me out. As we walked to our cars, Bill said, "I'm not Jewish, but the name of this place comes from a Jewish theologian." I pretended I didn't already know about Buber and asked him which of his books he would recommend I read first.

"*I and Thou*," he said. He stopped walking, turned to face me. "If I'm not treating another person as a *thou*, then I'm not on the narrow ridge. If I'm not treating you as a *thou* then I'm not on the narrow ridge. If I'm seeing the natural world as an it, instead of a *thou*, then I'm not on the narrow ridge."

He got into his truck and led me down winding roads. When he reached an intersection he pulled a quick U-turn. I rolled down the window to thank him, and he shouted, "Left, then straight, then left!" We drove off in separate directions, Bill turning back to Narrow Ridge while I headed for the city, lush green farmland unfurling on either side of the road along the way.

In the morning, I called Colin from my hotel bed and heard about how James excitedly pointed out steam—a word he'd learned from watching *Thomas the Tank Engine*—rising from his scrambled eggs that morning. I felt a weird ache over missing these small revelations. Until recently, when I asked James who mama was, he pointed to his own chest. But one night in the bath, a month or so before my trip, I asked him who mama was and he pointed to me for the first time. It seemed he'd only just begun differentiating between my body and his. For me, at least, it was an uneasy rift.

When we hung up the phone, I sat in my room with a paper cup of hotel coffee, still puzzling through my feelings about my dad and my son, faith and the church. I wrote in my journal: "What did I want for James? Wednesday nights in a fellowship hall, a long line of fluorescent-lit casseroles? Or the sense of never being fully alone in the world?" When I was a kid, I felt loved by God—or felt, in fact, that God was the sensation of belovedness. This is what I feel, now, as a parent, watching James receive the world, piece by piece. I remember what I love as I offer it to him; the world becomes precious to me all over again.

I checked out of the hotel and drove west for four hours, tendrils of mist snaking along the mountain ridges. I passed a stretch of pretty farmhouses sitting along a creek and parked my car at the trailhead of Larkspur Conservation, consulting the hand-painted map posted at the entry, before I began the hike up the rocky path, passing moss-covered boulders and mature stands of trees. John Christian Phifer, Larkspur's director, found me as I made my way up.

John Christian is one of the rare people who got into natural burial directly from conventional burial, after fifteen years spent working as a mortician in a funeral home. He has tightly coiled curly hair, a boyish smile, and a delightful West Tennessee accent that sounds just like home to me. He has talked to a lot of reporters, and was featured in a documentary, *Bury Me at Taylor Hollow*, that toured independent film festivals before premiering on PBS. When I asked him about what led him to become a mortician, he told me a story I'd read verbatim in news articles and profiles: As a child he provided elaborate burial rituals for dead animals he found.

While at Ramsey Creek the hiking trails were lined on either side with mounded graves, at Larkspur, at first, I didn't see any. We were walking in silence through a windswept meadow when John Christian turned and said, with no small measure of glee, "You just walked past two graves and didn't even know it!" We peered into tangled masses of dried native grasses; squinting, I could just make out the graves' numbered metal markers tacked into the ground. This is the goal of natural burial at a place like Larkspur—to return, to meld, to disappear into the place where you are planted.

We paused at the grave of a young mother who had died a year earlier, from brain cancer. For her funeral, and for many others, John Christian went all out, dyeing prayer flags with tea leaves, laying hundreds of flowers in a beautiful ombre display at the bottom of the grave. Hoping to better understand his attraction to death care, I asked whether it had something to do with this kind of ritual. "Yeah," he said. "I think so." He whacked at a patch of tall grass with a long stick.

He seemed much more comfortable speaking about death care and the funeral industry at large. Listing the environmental, spiritual, and financial benefits of natural burial, he says, "It just makes sense." When people talk about why they chose to get involved with natural burial, they often say some version of this: It just makes sense. After all, this is the way humans have put their loved ones to rest for millennia. What's radical about natural burial is not that it's innovative or new, but that it is a return to a wisdom that's been lost.

Any pretense of an interview broke down quickly once I left John Christian to meet up with Kellye Parr. When Kellye's mother was diagnosed with pancreatic cancer, she told her daughter that she wanted her grave to be marked by a native tree. Kellye wondered if she'd have to search for cemeteries on the West Coast. But then she heard about Larkspur, less than an hour away from her home in Nashville. Kellye drove her mother into the meadow, where she picked out her burial plot from the passenger seat of the car. When I asked Kellye if she would show me her mother's grave, she hesitated, biting her bottom lip. "I lose track of it sometimes, depending on the season," she said. "This place changes so much."

We walked along the outer edge of the meadow, peering into the tall grass. I worried, for a second, that we wouldn't be able to find the grave. "Here she is," Kellye said finally, and I followed her to a grave marked by a burr oak sapling and a rock on the ground with her mother's name engraved into it. From where we stood, I could see, now, the graves that John Christian had pointed out to me: a cremated mother and baby, buried together; a twelve-year-old child; a father whose middle-aged sons drove his body here in a pickup truck and played a couple songs on the guitar before lowering him into the earth. Standing there with Kellye, swaying a bit in the quiet, it felt rare, and sacred, to be surrounded by such evident care.

Kellye and I wandered the meadow, circling a small pond, walking slowly while we talked. When we came to the subject of religion, she told me about her last Sunday in church. As the congregation read a prayer in droning unison, she thought to herself, "I can't say these words one more time," and she got up and left and never went back. I found myself telling her the same story I'd told Matt Kelley at Grace

Church: the Christmas Eve service, my first time in a church since my father retired, when I cried every time the pipe organ bellowed or we bowed our heads in prayer. It still confounded me.

"You've experienced a death," Kellye said. "But you don't yet have a ritual for grieving it."

When I'd told Matt about the Christmas Eve service, the story seemed to demonstrate a longing for continuation; it implied that I was on a journey that would lead me back in some way to the place where I began. In my insistence on finding some coherence, I'd managed to avoid seeing—and grieving—an ending for what it really was. I'd grown up with the rare gift of a religious community in which I felt safe and loved, with a faith that was nurtured within and alongside my doubts. My life had been utterly shaped around walking into church and seeing my father in the doorway, and now there was no church, anywhere in the world, where I could find him on Sunday morning.

For more than forty years, my father had written each of his sermons by hand. With each stack of yellowing paper tossed in the fire, he seemed to be erasing vast swaths of history and memory that didn't belong only to him. But when I told Kellye about my father burning his sermons, a sight that had so troubled me, Kellye just smiled. "See, he's finding grief rituals of his own," she said. "Now you just need to find yours."

The fears I had—of loss, and change, and time slipping through my fingers—seemed to be answered by the meadow Kellye and I walked through, where all around us bodies were disintegrating bit by bit, just as we are supposed to. The Book of Common Prayer promises that "Life is changed, not ended," and when I think about the decay of the body—the cells breaking down, the body's nutrients returned to the soil by microbes and bacteria, to be consumed by insects and fungi and be integrated into the life cycle of the land—it seems clear that, no matter what happens to a person's soul, the body lives on for who knows how long in the world around us: Heaven is just a breath away.

As I left Larkspur and drove to the hotel where I'd spend a final night before returning home, I thought about a story that Kimberley Campbell told me about the way her husband, Billy, digs graves at Ramsey Creek. When they first began burying people, Billy used a backhoe, but found it too disruptive. He quickly switched to digging by hand, in sections: first removing the forest floor, then the topsoil, then the clay and rocks of the subsoil. These different layers are rolled up and kept separate, and once the body is placed in the grave, the layers are placed back in the grave in order, unfurled like a blanket, one at a time.

Billy places a layer of wood chips and combustible materials around the body, to make space for air and microbes and fungi. He invites decay, welcomes it in. This close attention to the individual ecosystem of each grave means that the body's nutrients are absorbed into the ground more easily, and the land that was disturbed in the process of digging the grave is able to restore itself more quickly. But mostly the image that stays with me is of a person being tucked so lovingly into this world.

THE LIFE EVERLASTING

COMING INTO ARKANSAS FROM Memphis, casinos and hospitals are the only structures that look permanent. Otherwise, there are corrugated metal garages and weather-beaten sheds, parking lots full of farming equipment, and miles of sunbaked soybean, rice, and cotton fields. We drive in the shadow of billboards promising to *make farming great again*, or *end veteran suicide*, punctuated by the looming triple-Xs of adult superstores.

Whenever I asked people what they knew about Brinkley, Arkansas, I heard of wedding gowns and duck hunting. Both are true: The Low's Bridal and Formal outlet store draws brides-to-be from around the region to shop in "Arkansas's Largest Bridal Shop," while the swamps surrounding Brinkley, situated on the Mississippi Flyway, are thick with duck hunters every winter. When I clicked Brinkley's location tag on Instagram, I saw women holding up ubiquitous white garment bags, their newly purchased wedding gowns zipped safely inside, alongside camouflaged men holding up freshly-shot ducks, necks dangling, feathers still slick with blood and swampwater.

When, in 2005, the Cornell Lab of Ornithology announced that at least one ivory-billed woodpecker, long considered extinct, had been observed in the swamps just outside town, Brinkley was quick to capitalize. I'd heard there were signs along the highway welcoming travelers to Brinkley, announcing it was "The Home of the Ivory-Billed Woodpecker." I'd heard that the town built a convention center to host an annual ivory-billed woodpecker conference, that salons offered ivory-bill haircuts, and that there were ivory-bill burgers and lawn signs and gift shops and mascots.

But there were no signs of the town's ivory-billed fervor when I visited, sixteen years after the ornithologist Tim Gallagher, then the editor of Cornell's *Living Bird* magazine, claimed he saw an ivory-bill fly past his canoe. "Nothing symbolizes what we have lost more than the ivory-billed woodpecker," Gallagher later wrote in his book, *The Grail Bird: The Rediscovery of the Ivory-billed Woodpecker.* "Just to think that this bird has made it into the twenty-first century gives me chills. It's as though a funeral shroud has been pulled back, giving us a brief glimpse of a living bird, rising like Lazarus from the grave."

The ivory-bill has been called the *Lord God Bird,* for its massive size, and the *The Grail Bird,* for the fervor with which people seek it out. It is also considered a *Ghost Bird,* for the way it refuses classification—hovering on the murky edge between existence and extinction. But Gallagher's new name for the ivory-bill, *Lazarus Bird,* stood out to me. The name references the story from the Gospel of John, in which Jesus resurrects Lazarus, the brother of Martha and Mary Magdalene, four days after he died.

Unlike Christ, Lazarus did not appear briefly on earth only to ascend to heaven. Instead, Lazarus came back from the dead and just kept on living, his life relatively unchanged except for the fact that he must one day die again, and return, forever, to whatever world held him those four days in the tomb. In paintings depicting his resurrection, Lazarus is shown emerging from the tomb with strips of cloth hanging off his thin frame, his face bewildered and pale.

Growing up in the church, I was never sure what to do with resurrection. My father's faith didn't emphasize the idea that Christ died in exchange for my salvation, or that Christ's believers would themselves be raised from the dead, but these beliefs were everywhere, in the hymns we sang, in the creed we recited by heart every Sunday: *I believe in the Holy Spirit, the holy catholic church, the communion of saints, the forgiveness of sins, the resurrection of the body, and the life everlasting.*

From my seat in the pews, the promise of everlasting life rang hollow. I did not truly expect that the decomposed bodies of believers would one day be reconstituted, nor did I see this as a desirable future for myself or the people I loved. But metaphorical interpretations of resurrection also seemed to fall short: a body raised symbolically from the dead is, after all, still very much dead. In graduate school, I read about Thomas Jefferson's excision of miracles, including the resurrection, from his Bible with a sense of relief. The stories I couldn't believe literally, and couldn't understand figuratively, could be simply cut away. But as I've grown older, these stories resist my neat excision. To dismiss resurrection entirely, act as if this part of the story was a simple error that could be erased, feels increasingly fraught: Why did faith matter if it did not transform real bodies, real lives, here on earth?

As I drove through Brinkley, I stopped in the parking lot of the Arkansas Game and Fish Commission's regional office to see a mural painted on the building's side: A collection of native birds, mammals, and fish congregating alongside a winding river. Among the turkeys, white-tailed deer, and alligators, there were no ivory-bills sweeping through the leafy canopy or stripping bark from trees. Next door, the sign outside the rotary club announced cheerfully, WE ARE PROMOTING POSITIVE EMOTIONS!—and, less cheerfully—STAY ALIVE!

In the parking lot of a Kroger that seemed to have been otherwise unchanged since the 1970s, I saw a neat row of Tesla charging stations, the sleek white and red machines totally incongruous with the grocery store's vintage exterior. Two Teslas were parked there, charging, one with custom Anti-Biden vanity plates. On Facebook, the Brinkley News Network excitedly announced that the construction of the charging stations was nearing completion: "This means that Brinkley will get more people with electric cars that are traveling on I-40. HUGE WIN!!!" The post was accompanied by a hashtag, #brinkleyisnotdead.

Where it was once thought that the resurrection of the ivory-bill might bring with it the resurrection of Brinkley, it seemed the town itself was no longer hoping for rebirth or renewal. With little hope for resurrection, Brinkley's goal seems to have shifted: to *promote positive emotions*; to *stay alive,* to be *not dead.*

Many people considered the ivory-bill extinct by 1924, when ornithologist Jim Tanner and his wife Nancy saw a pair of them in Florida. A decade later, when Tanner joined an expedition of ornithologists trekking across the South, he took vivid photographs of a fledgling ivory-bill, and the team made the only known recording of the ivory-bill's call, using massive equipment they lugged through dense forests on mule-drawn wagons. Tanner's doctoral thesis on the ivory-bill, published by the National Audubon Society in the 1930s, estimated there were only twelve ivory-bill pairs left.

The last universally accepted ivory-bill sighting was in 1944, when the Audubon Field Guide illustrator Don Eckelberry spent two weeks along Louisiana's Tensas River, in what was once an 80,000-acre tract of woods owned by the Singer Sewing Machine Company. When the company sold its logging rights, the Audubon Society tried, unsuccessfully, to intervene. As the forest was being logged, Eckelberry followed and painted the last ivory-bill he could find, a female bird that he observed flying through a mangled, cutover forest, landing on her roosting tree at sunset, and calling out with no answer. People have reported sightings often since then—from Louisiana's Atchafalaya Basin, and Georgia's Okefenokee Swamp, to South Carolina's Santee Basin—but none of these sightings could be confirmed by subsequent searches.

By the time I bought a worn, used copy of *The Grail Bird,* Tim Gallagher's account of his ivory-bill sighting was already more than fifteen years old, but I tore through it like it was a mystery novel. Gallagher originally set out to write about people who claimed to have seen an ivory-bill, and in his conversations with birders and ornithologists, Gallagher sensed occasional glimmers of hope that the bird might still exist, sometimes by parsing individual words: When Gallagher interviewed Nancy Tanner, she spoke about ivory-bills in the present tense, "as though she thought that they definitely still existed."

Most of the reported sightings Gallagher investigated were decades old—too distant to inspire much hope for the bird's continued existence—until he heard about a man named Gene Sparling who claimed to have seen an ivory-bill in Arkansas just a week earlier. Gallagher and his friend and fellow birder Bobby Harrison met up with Sparling in a scrawny stretch of swamp bordered by a humming highway overpass. A few days into their search, a large, black-and-white woodpecker appeared from a side channel and flew through the trees in front of their boat. Gallagher and Harrison "both cried out simultaneously," Gallagher wrote, "'Ivory-bill!'" Before they spoke to each other about what they'd seen, Gallagher and Harrison stopped to take field notes separately, writing nearly identical descriptions of a large black bird with white marks on the trailing edge of its wings. "No knowledgeable person could have misidentified it," Gallagher wrote. When Harrison called his wife and told her the news, he broke down in tears.

Gallagher knew they'd need evidence, if not inarguable proof, before they could tell anyone of their sighting. Those who claim to have seen an ivory-bill are deemed believable or not by a chorus of experts who have themselves never seen an ivory-bill, and who, more often than not, doubt that the bird still exists. Paradoxically, the people whose sightings are the most readily believed tend to be those who are the most tentative, telling only a select few about their sighting, or doing so anonymously, or hesitating to claim with too much certainty what they saw. The more one doubts one's own experience, hides it from the public, the more believable one's sighting seems. But when Gallagher returned to Cornell from the swamps of Arkansas, he insisted that he was "absolutely certain" about what he saw.

Soon teams of students and volunteers were descending on the Arkansas swamps, hoping to find evidence that could corroborate Gallagher's sighting. But when the Cornell Lab of Ornithology announced the ivory-billed woodpecker's rediscovery in the Big Woods area of Arkansas, a year after Gallagher's initial sighting, they were armed with meager evidence: a blurry, four-second video of a bird in flight, several brief sightings by members of the search team who had not been able to get a photograph, and an acoustic recording they claimed to be the distinctive double-rap of the ivory-bill. The team published a cover story in *Science* magazine and held a press conference with representatives from the U.S. Department of the Interior to announce that the ivory-billed woodpecker had been discovered in Arkansas.

The Department of the Interior announced that $2.1 million would be devoted to conservation and habitat restoration efforts that might lead to the ivory-bill's recovery. In addition, three groups from Arkansas and Mississippi received nearly $800,000 for private lands conservation, restoring bottomland hardwood wetlands, implementing forestry practices like prescribed fires, and reforesting previously cleared land. The ivory-bill's rediscovery led the Nature Conservancy to accelerate their work in the Big Woods area, protecting thousands of acres of land and planting millions of trees. The ivory-bill's rediscovery was also highlighted on USDA promotional materials to encourage participation in programs like the Wetland Reserve Program, which paid farmers and landowners to restore wetlands and bottomland forests on private land.

In the final pages of *The Grail Bird*, Gallagher writes about visiting Arkansas in the months following his sighting, as teams of volunteers and full-time searchers began combing through the swamps, looking for signs. As he paddled his canoe through the Bayou DeView, Gallagher thought of all the people who "were scorned for daring to believe that the ivory-billed woodpecker still lived. Surely the work we have done in Arkansas, the rediscovery of the species, has vindicated them, I thought. Or has it? Who knows? If no additional evidence of the ivory-bill is found this field season, we may well join the ranks of ornithological pariahs."

Shortly after Cornell's announcement, the renowned illustrator David Sibley and three other authors published an article in *Science* arguing that none of the characteristics shown in the four-second video ruled out the possibility that the video shows a pileated woodpecker. An article in the *New York Times* described the hair-splitting, endlessly arguable details of the controversy as "downright Talmudic": the Cornell group claimed that the white patches visible on the bird's wings in the four-second video were the top of ivory-bill wings, while skeptics claimed these white patches were the bottom of pileated wings.

The audio recordings also came under scrutiny: John Fitzpatrick, the Executive Director of the Cornell Lab of Ornithology, acknowledged that the sounds they recorded might not have been ivory-bills, after all, but blue jays mimicking the ivory-bill audio recordings that searchers played in hopes they might provoke an ivory-bill's response. A year after Cornell's announcement, ornithologist Jerome Jackson published a critique of Cornell's findings in *The Auk*, dismissing their claims as "faith-based ornithology."

By 2010, the Cornell Lab of Ornithology had ended its search for the ivory-bill with no solid evidence of the bird's return. An article in the *Cornell Chronicle* began, "They have searched the old-growth forests of the Carolinas, the swamps of Arkansas, the woods of Alabama and Mississippi, and now the vast river of grass, mangrove, cypress and wildlife that make up the Florida Everglades. But if the legendary ivory-billed woodpecker still inhabits any corner of the southeast United States, the bird remains—by humans, at least—unseen and unheard."

Growing up in Memphis, just across the river from Arkansas, I never had a sense of what "nature" meant, here—no idea what this area would have looked like long ago. But sometimes, in the strange empty stretches of land beyond the outskirts of town, between suburb and strip malls, I'd catch sight of a flooded stretch of woods along the highway, trees jutting out from standing water, and feel a thrum of recognition, a sense that I'd glimpsed what this part of the world once looked like, or might still look like, somewhere.

Because it was so remote, much of southeastern Arkansas's bottomland forests remained untouched throughout the 19th century, until the construction of railroads allowed loggers access to vast tracts of old-growth pine, cypress, and hardwood trees. Brinkley itself came into being when a rail line was built connecting Memphis and Little Rock.

Driving beyond Brinkley to the swamps outside its edges, it was hard to imagine a forest, where now there is none—hard to see the fields we drove past as an absence of something that could have been here in its place. I tried to conjure the oaks: nuttall and pin; water and willow, that once would have formed a thick, shady canopy as far as the eye can see. Instead, cotton plants popped up in ditches and front yards; crop dusters flew low over the highway; vultures hunched over a deer carcass smeared across the road's shoulder.

Almost every inch of the Big Woods area has been logged at least once. On the day I spent canoeing a section of the Bayou deView, paddling past bald cypress, water oaks, and tupelo, I tried to imagine the trees as tiny seedlings, fifty or a hundred years ago, unfurling their leaves during a long dry stretch. Did they sprout around the stumps of the trees that had been logged years before?

Part of me resists mentally overlaying loss onto every tree, placing human destruction at the center of the story of this place, which has existed long before humans and will exist long after us. Part of me also wants to resist neat narratives of death and resurrection, stories that, in their insistence on life everlasting, seem to skip over mourning what has been lost.

In a 1955 lecture, the theologian Paul Tillich said that resurrection "has for many people the connotation of dead bodies leaving their graves or other fanciful images." To Tillich, resurrection did not refer to any literal event, whether it was Christ's return from the tomb or any future event in which believers would be raised from the dead. Instead, he said, "Resurrection means the victory of the New state of things, the New Being born out of the death of the Old." Resurrection was the ongoing "power of the New Being" to transform death into life in the present moment. "Resurrection happens *now,*" Tillich wrote, "or it does not happen at all."

Tillich's ideas might have sounded new to some listeners, and he is still occasionally declared a liberal heretic by some conservative

Christians. But he was expressing a line of thinking that, by many accounts, predated the literal interpretation of Jesus's resurrection. In the early years after Christ's death, some of Christ's followers believed that spirit and matter were irreconcilably separate entities, and that Christ only *seemed* to have a physical body but was in fact a purely spiritual being: He was not incarnated in a physical human body as an infant, and he did not die, or return from the dead, in a physical human body either. These beliefs—called "docetic," from a Greek word meaning "to seem"—were absorbed into the larger, so-called gnostic movement, and surfaced in texts written in the second and third century following Christ's death.

Basilides, an Egyptian gnostic teacher, said, "Salvation belongs to the soul alone." The Roman gnostic Valentinus argued that it was "impossible" for the physical body to "partake of salvation." The Gnostic Gospel of Philip reads, "Those that say they will die first and then rise are in error." In *The Treatise on Resurrection,* resurrection occurs in the present, as an experience of enlightenment, rather than a discrete event in either the past or the future.

Christ's death and resurrection as physical, literal events were most famously defended in the second century by Tertullian and Iranaeus, two prominent figures in early Christianity, who saw God's power to resurrect the dead mirrored and foretold by God's creation of the universe. Resurrection was reflected in the natural world that God created. Tertullian wrote that all of creation "has an instinct for renewal." Iranaeus argued that "God's desire is always to bring things to, or back to, life." "To put it in one word, the whole creation is recurrent," Tertullian wrote. "Nothing exists for the first time."

This is the logic of resurrection that I can't quite shake, the internal, embodied rhythms of the earth's predictable cycles lulling me into believing there will always be more: That when the sun disappears for the night, it will always reappear the next morning, illuminating the crinkled horizon; that the brittle cold and dark of winter will yield to the lengthening days of a sun-warmed spring; that what we lose will come back to us, in whatever new forms. Some part of me believes that the world will continue on, each day dying and revealing a new day in its wake, with no record-scratch, no finality, no real, permanent end.

Extinction seems somehow more final than death itself, reminding us not only of our own individual endings, but the fact that all we've known will one day cease to be. E.O. Wilson has written of the finality of extinction: "Oblivion, absolute oblivion, is the one image the human mind cannot accept or even fully conceive. Deeper than despair, more terrifying than death, is the thought that everything in time will disappear, that all we have been and will become will leave no trace whatsoever," he writes. But there is "a different kind of immortality," he writes, to be found in "those remnants of the natural world we have not yet destroyed."

Lately, something about the elegiac tone with which we increasingly hear and speak and write of the natural world—in this era of mass extinction, biodiversity loss, and increasingly frequent and extreme natural disasters—has driven the resurrection to the front of my mind. It seems possible that our concepts of conservation and preservation—of "saving" the world from the myriad catastrophes it faces and "restoring" the places we've lost—rely in part on the narrative of resurrection, of bringing a dead thing back to life, and with it, saving ourselves.

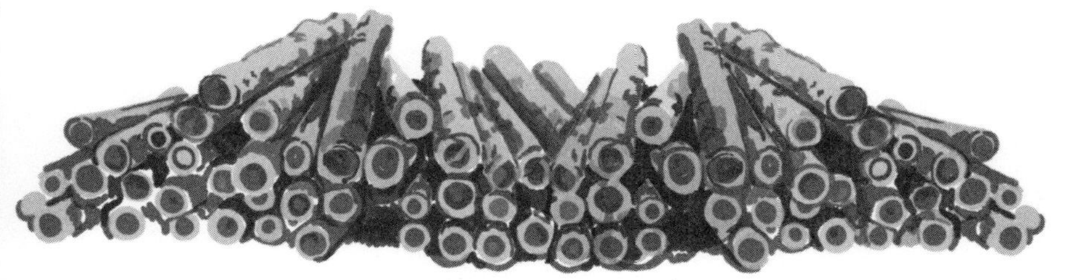

Over the past decade, the languages of faith and science have collided as advances in synthetic biology and genetic engineering have made it possible to bring approximate versions of certain species back from extinction. In 2016, both the International Union for Conservation of Nature and the University of California in Santa Barbara published guidelines for de-extinction. That same year, researchers at Trent State University published their findings on the "resurrection potential" of the Carolina parakeet, the passenger pigeon, and the ivory-billed woodpecker, concluding that the ivory-bill would be the best candidate of the three. In 2021, a Harvard University genetics professor started a de-extinction company with $15 million dollars in funding and a splashy website that declares de-extinction the solution to our ecological collapse.

Some argue that rather than trying to undo the past by resurrecting species that are already extinct, scientists should instead invest their time, research, and resources into preventing further, future extinctions just on the horizon. And the threat of coming extinctions is dire. A 2019 report published in *Science* found that, in less than fifty years, the bird population in the U.S. and Canada had fallen by nearly 30 percent, or three billion individual birds. Insect-eaters, forest-dwellers, and migratory birds had all seen population drops, but grassland birds had suffered the largest losses, with more than 700 million individual grassland birds gone.

Stories about decreasing bird populations have been spreading around the country. In West Virginia, where eastern meadowlarks used to be a common sight, the birds have begun to disappear. In Tennessee, where the bobwhite quail is the state's official game bird, the bird's populations have plummeted due to the loss of farmland. In Florida, where 90 percent of the state's roseate spoonbills once nested in Florida Bay, lately only 10 percent were showing up each year. In a time of ongoing present-day losses, it seems strange to expend resources on bringing back our long-gone dead.

Some proponents of de-extinction argue that resurrecting specific species could fill holes in the ecosystems they've left behind, righting some of the wrongs left in extinction's wake. But whatever environmental problems de-extinction might address, de-extinction itself seems like an attempt to address the moral problem of extinction, a way of repenting for all the ways extinction indicts us. Creating genetic near-replicas of extinct species is not the same as "resurrecting" the actual, individual lives that were lost, and won't magically restore those species' former habitats either.

Ivory-billed woodpeckers were themselves resurrection creatures. While smaller woodpeckers feasted on insects living in long-dead trees, ivory-billed woodpeckers, with their massive heads and beaks, depended on large amounts of newly dead trees, from which they would peel large strips of bark to access the beetles and larvae living underneath. Ivory-bills left holes in trees that other birds and animals would use to nest, and they sped up the decomposition of dead trees. When these trees finally fell, the open spaces they left behind allowed sunlight to pierce the forest's thick canopy, making room for new life, helping saplings to grow and fill the spaces these felled trees left behind. Gallagher referred to ivory-bills as "disaster species" for the way they thrived on forests that had just been through a traumatic event, like logging, a hurricane, or saltwater incursion, anything that left a trail of newly-dead trees in its wake. They would have been the perfect creatures for our time, at home in a world of change and disruption.

While the synoptic gospels—Matthew, Mark, and Luke—all cover the same period of time, telling roughly the same stories in roughly the same order, it's clear, from its opening lines, that John's gospel operates on a distinctly cosmic scale. Where Matthew and Luke both begin with Jesus's birth, and Mark begins with Jesus's baptism, John begins at the beginning of time itself: "In the beginning was the Word, and the Word was with God, and the Word was God."

In addition to leaving out some of the stories found in the synoptic gospels, John also included stories not found in any other gospel. The story of Lazarus's resurrection appears only in John, as does the characterization of the apostle Thomas as "Doubting Thomas." And while other gospels identify Jesus as a great teacher, a leader, and even the Messiah, John is the only of the four gospel accounts that directly claims that Jesus *is* God; that Jesus and God are one in the same.

As the New Testament was being codified, other gnostic and apocryphal texts were declared heretical and ordered to be destroyed. Elaine Pagels's 1989 book *The Gnostic Gospels* describes an Egyptian man named Muhammad 'Alí al-Sammán finding a cache of leather-bound papyrus codices in 1945. The texts had been hidden in a clay jar and buried near a cave. His mother burned much of the papyrus in her oven as kindling, and most of the remaining books were sold at a black market in Cairo, but eventually fifty-two apocryphal texts, including the Gospel of Thomas, the Gospel of Philip, the Gospel of Truth, and the Gospel of Mary Magdalene, were recovered. These 1,500-year-old Coptic translations of the original, older texts had likely been hidden by someone, perhaps a monk from a nearby monastery who couldn't bear to destroy them. These apocryphal texts seem marginal to those of us accustomed to the books codified as the Bible we know today. But, Pagels argues, the devotion shown to these texts by whoever decided to bury them and keep them safe reveals how much they once meant.

Some scholars believe that John's gospel and Thomas's gospel each had their own devoted followers—Johannine Christians and Thomas Christians—that formed rival communities. In the Thomas tradition, Jesus was not a resurrected God; instead, Jesus offered teachings and wisdom that could lead followers to their own interior resurrections, which could come during their own lives, not after death. Rather than "believing" in Jesus as God, followers of the Gospel of Thomas and other Gnostic texts were encouraged to deeply know themselves, in order to "bring forth that which is within them."

Any time I dip into the Gospel of Thomas, I find it a jarring, emotional experience to see familiar characters recast in such different light. These gospels offer glimpses of another, possible version of Christianity, and the discovery of the Nag Hammadi texts is often interpreted as a kind of rediscovery of what was lost.

But some scholars refute this interpretation of the Nag Hammadi story. Philip Jenkins, a professor at Baylor University, argues that Gnostic texts had been discovered as much as a century earlier, and that their teachings had, in many cases, been thoroughly absorbed into the larger Christian culture. He writes, "It's a clear story—a myth-of concealment and near-miraculous rediscovery, even a kind of resurrection, and if it seems too good to be true, that is just what it is." I don't know. I'm not a biblical scholar. But the texts have meant a lot to me.

The outlier stories found in the Gospel of John, which are not included in any of the synoptic gospels, serve to underscore John's overarching message that Christ was one with God. The story of Lazarus's resurrection, for example, not only provides a reason for Jesus's arrest and his execution, but also serves as proof that Jesus, with the power to raise the dead to life, was God himself.

The character "Doubting Thomas" comes from John's gospel, and seems like a particularly pointed critique of Thomas Christians. In the other gospels, Christ's followers experience a healthy dose of doubt surrounding his resurrection; in the Gospel of Luke, *all* of the disciples are in disbelief when the resurrected Christ appears before them. But in the Gospel of John, alone, Thomas is the only disciple who doubts Christ's bodily resurrection, telling the other disciples that he must touch Christ's open wounds before he will believe.

In John's gospel, Jesus finally appears to Thomas a week after he originally appeared to the other disciples. He addresses Thomas's need for proof directly, telling him to touch his wounds. But it seems that sight is enough proof for Thomas, after all, who cries out, "My Lord and my God!" Then Jesus scolds him, saying, "Because you have seen me, you have believed; blessed are those who have not seen and yet have believed."

To many, this moment in John's gospel, when Thomas finally professes belief that Jesus is God, is the triumphant climax of the entire story of Christ's resurrection. Belief, in John's Gospel, is what the "good news" demands, and in this way John's narrative refutes the Thomas tradition, which did not "believe" in Jesus the way Johannine Christians did.

Orthodox church leaders used John's gospel to codify the belief in Christ's divinity and the physical resurrection of Christ and his followers, and to promote the spiritual wisdom of believing without seeing. In *The Gnostic Gospels,* Pagels writes, "In place of Thomas's cryptic sayings, John offers a simple formula, revealed through the story of Jesus's life, death, and resurrection: 'God loves you; believe, and be saved.'"

In the years since the Cornell Lab of Ornithology's announcement, the controversy over the ivory-bill's rediscovery has often been boiled down to a binary argument between skeptics and believers. And though the skeptics may have more ground to stand on, the believers seem way more fun. In the 2009 documentary, *Ghost Bird,* the skeptics are shown in sterile labs, pontificating over their collections of taxidermied birds, while the believers suit up and head out into the swamp, day after day, their eyes trained on the trees.

When Gallagher interviewed experts to hear which reported sightings they believed and which they doubted, he asked each of these experts what he called "the big question"—*do they believe there are any ivory-bills left in the world?* In Gallagher's tautology, people who doubt that the ivory-bill still exists are predisposed to dismiss reported sightings, while belief in the bird's continued existence becomes evidence for the bird's survival. Whenever Gallagher repeats "the big question," asking experts what they doubt and what they believe, I am reminded of the Bible's own definition of faith as "the substance of things hoped for, the evidence of things not seen."

Unlike Gallagher, I didn't ask outright whether the people I spoke with believed the ivory-bill still exists, or whether they believed that it even existed when Cornell announced it had been seen in the Big Woods. Instead, I took note of the way one Arkansas Game and Fish Commission employee said "Oh, boy," when I asked about the ivory-bill over the phone; or the way a local forester took a deep breath when I mentioned the bird's name. I noticed the way one U.S. Fish and Wildlife Service employee, who I will call Amanda, referred to the "quote-unquote discovery," or the "so-called discovery" of the ivory-bill back when she was a young biologist working in coastal South Carolina, and her life was uprooted when she was reassigned to the Cache River National Wildlife Refuge, to spend months searching the swamps for signs of the ivory-bill.

Specifically, she was looking for nesting cavities, which Fitzpatrick said would be "the next big clue" that ivory-bills might persist in the Big Woods. At first, Amanda was pretty excited about the search. She even suited up in an ivory-bill costume at festivals and conferences. The ivory-bill was being described as a keystone species, or a creature upon which the larger ecosystem depends. Amanda thought the ivory-bill could harness attention and resources that would help conserve and preserve precious remnants of southern bottomland hardwood forests.

"But," Amanda said, "the longer I stayed in Arkansas, the more I realized that maybe there probably wasn't a bird there." She and her colleagues did see a lot of striking pileated woodpeckers, with unique white markings: "We all saw birds that were mostly white or white where they should have been black, but they were clearly pileated."

The birds were leucistic, she said, a trait which is similar to albinism but causes only a partial loss of pigmentation. The white patches could have made the pileateds, which typically have black wings, look more like ivory-bills, which typically have white feathers on the trailing edges of their wings. I asked if the ornithologists from Cornell would have known about leucism.

"I'm sure they knew about that trait," she said. "But they may not have realized at the time that there was clearly this pretty continuous trait in that population of pileateds."

Amanda didn't want to question anyone else's experience. "But the more I saw those pileateds, with what seemed like a pretty common genetic trait for woodpeckers in that area, I started to think that's what they saw. That's the explanation that occurred to me as I tried to make sense of the story."

"I have to use rational thought and scientific training," she said. "There are people with great conviction who say they saw what they believe to be an ivory-bill. I wasn't there and I don't believe it's my place to question them. But we have to have some solid evidence. Right now we're headed down a path with no solid evidence."

I wondered if seeing the ivory-bill as a proxy for its own habitat might be part of the problem. As a keystone species for southeastern bottomland forests, the ivory-bill had become the main character of a winding, complicated story. And for those devoted to the ivory-bill—and its habitat—a public declaration that the ivory-bill was finally, irrevocably, hopelessly gone might seem like a death knell for the habitat too. Amanda told me that the use of keystone species was "a bedrock of wildlife management." But what if efforts to save a specific keystone species fails? When the salvation of an entire habitat relies on a single species, and that species doesn't make it, how can we then widen our view?

In March of 2021, Gallagher and Harrison appeared on CBS *Sunday Morning,* canoeing slowly between tupelo and cypress trees in the Bayou deView, affixing decoy ivory-bills to tree trunks. Harrison talked about how more vulnerable bottomland habitat could be protected if they were able to finally offer proof of the ivory-bill's continued existence. The ivory-bill, he said, is "really a symbol of what's been lost."

Six months later, the U.S. Fish and Wildlife Service recommended that twenty-three species, including the ivory-billed woodpecker, be removed from federal protection under the Endangered Species Act and declared extinct. This announcement seemed to have no impact on Fitzpatrick or Gallagher's belief that the bird might still persist—or their belief that belief, itself, might still be used for some good. In the wake of the extinction announcement, Gallagher wrote in *Audubon* encouraging ivory-bill skeptics and believers, alike, to submit a comment to the U.S. Fish and Wildlife Service during the 60-day comment period. "What's the hurry to declare the bird extinct anyway?" Gallagher wrote. "Is any harm being done if people have to take a little extra time and thought before clearing vital southern forest habitat to make way for fields of rice and soybeans? These forests are far too important for all the plant and animal species and other life forms that exist within them."

Fitzpatrick was quoted in *Politico*: "A bird this iconic, and this representative of the major old-growth forests of the southeast, keeping it on the list of endangered species keeps attention on it, keeps states thinking about managing habitat on the off chance it still exists." Gallagher shared the article on Twitter, adding, "The USFWS is making a huge mistake in declaring the Ivory-billed Woodpecker extinct." Later that day, Gallagher tweeted the cover of his book, *The Grail Bird,* with the caption, "The Ivory-bill lives!"

A few months later, I logged onto a U.S. Fish and Wildlife Service virtual public hearing on their intention to remove the ivory-billed woodpecker from the endangered species list and declare the bird extinct. The meeting began, somewhat absurdly, with a PowerPoint presentation on characteristics of the ivory-bill, which I noticed was read in the past tense: The bird *was* the largest woodpecker in the U.S. and the second largest in North America; the ivory-bill *was* black and white, with a chisel-shaped beak. As the presenter spoke, I scrolled through the list of 150 or so names at the top of the screen to see who was logged on, recognizing many of the usual characters: David Luneau, John Fitzpatrick, Bobby Harrison, Tim Gallagher. Over the course of two hours, attendees were called on, unmuted, and allowed to speak for two minutes each, making their case for whether the ivory-bill should be considered extinct or not.

One man made a passionate speech about protecting the ivory-bill's habitat in the face of increasing wood pellet production in the Southeast; a woman from Tallahassee spoke about the ivory-bill's sacred relationship with indigenous peoples; one man said that the ivory-bill would be worth 150 million dollars in ecotourism; another cited a single ivory-bill feather discovered in 1969. A guy who claimed to have spent "hours searching the websites" for proof of the ivory-bill's continued existence said that the resources devoted to the ivory-bill should "go to other, better birds." A disgruntled ornithologist used his allotted two minutes at the public hearing to complain that ivory-bill supporters "never get a fair hearing." When a skeptic complained about "eyewitness testimony" offered as evidence that the ivory-bill persists, another ornithologist argued, intensely but not incorrectly, that "we execute people in this country for eyewitness testimony."

I kept expecting to hear Tim Gallagher's voice, crackling over a bad connection, arguing why the ivory-bill should be left under federal protection. But I'm not sure, really, what I want from Gallagher. A public renunciation of his beliefs? Do I want him to fess up, admit that he doesn't believe the ivory-bill still actually exists, but he wants to use the possibility of the bird to protect habitat anyway? His unwavering faith has no perceptible cracks. Did he really still believe that an ivory-bill persisted somewhere—anywhere—in the southeast?

Gallagher never spoke at the public hearing, and I scrolled through the list of names several times to confirm that he was still there, somewhere, listening. But the more I imagined what he might say, the more certain I felt that I did not, in fact, want Gallagher to join the ranks of the nonbelievers, and that if he were to unmute himself and say, with a weary sigh, *all right, you've convinced me. There are no ivory-bills left,* I'd feel that admission as a kind of damnation, an irrevocable, irreversible loss.

A couple days after the public hearing, a staff person sent out an email that the recording had been uploaded to the U.S. Fish and Wildlife Service website. I noted, with some schadenfreudic glee, that the staff person had mistakenly copied—not blind-copied—all the people who registered for the hearing, so that we now had access to the email addresses of all the participants. A few days later, a different staff person sent out another email chiding the group for "less than civil discourse" that had started going on behind the scenes.

What is it about the ivory-bill, in particular, that inspires such passion and obsession? While other birds have gone officially extinct with the death of one last living example—like the last passenger pigeon, named Martha, who died at the Cincinnati Zoo in 1914, or Incas, the last Carolina parakeet, who died at the same zoo four years later—there was no singular, final ivory-bill to watch languish in an enclosure, its death providing the end date for the entire species. Until that happens, the ivory-bill can remain a tantalizing possibility, a reminder of the forests that once stretched across the South, teeming with emerald-green parakeets, red wolves, panthers, and flocks of passenger pigeons so large they blotted out the sun; forests of abundance unlike anything that remains today.

I wanted to see an ivory-bill, too, so I spent weeks searching online archives across the southeast, trying to figure out where a taxidermied specimen might be on view. After making a list of possibilities—museums in Louisiana and South Carolina, a library in Kentucky—I finally texted a friend who worked at a museum a few blocks from my house and asked if, by chance, they might have any taxidermied ivory-bills. *Yep!* he said, *Wanna come by on Thursday and take a look?*

When Thursday came, I made the less-than-five-minute drive to the museum as slowly as I could, trying not to arrive too early. My friend led me to their ivory-bill specimen, in a glass display case, situated in the darkest corner of the room. On either side of his case were taxidermied birds of prey, arranged in groups: owls huddled together in one display case, several hawk specimens in another. But the ivory-bill sat alone; no other woodpeckers nearby, no other ivory-bill companions in his display case.

Ivory-bills do not hold up well to taxidermy. There's not a nicer way to say it. They look awful. Perhaps it is their own karmic reproach, a kind of curse, their ragged stiff bodies a shameful reminder that the preserved specimen can never replicate a living bird. This ivory-bill, unlike some that I viewed online, was at least recognizable, posed against a tree branch as if he was frozen mid-climb. But his bill was turning orange, and his feathers looked patchy and damaged. The placard identifying him declared he was *presumed extinct.*

Helen Macdonald writes that endangered animals face a diminishment in meaning that goes beyond their dwindling population numbers: "When animals become so rare that their impact on humans is negligible, their ability to generate new meanings lessens," she writes, "and it is then that they come to stand for another human notion: our own moral failings in our relationship to the natural world."

I thought of the way Gallagher described the ivory-bill in *The Grail Bird,* as "a symbol of everything that has gone wrong with our relationship to the environment." I'd met that bird, the symbol, before. And here, sealed in a glass case, was the husk of what was once a living bird, real and concrete and representing only himself. No amount of de-extinction technology or rehabilitated ecosystems will do anything for the actual, innumerable ivory-billed woodpeckers who starved or died as their habitats splintered rapidly and they were cut off from mating partners and food sources, or who were shot and stuffed, their lifeless bodies lining curio cabinets and museum display cases. To conflate de-extinction with resurrection requires thinking of an ivory-bill as somehow representative, as a symbol or an idea, rather than as an individual bird, with a singular life.

The taxidermied ivory-bill reminded me of the idea that some words are untranslatable, lacking an easy one-to-one comparison crossing from one language to another. He looked almost entirely unrelated to the pair of ivory-bills captured in Arthur Allen's 1935 video, their quick, jerky movements almost too fast to see as they moved around a tree trunk, bobbing into and out of a nesting hole. The stuffed museum specimen didn't look like something that had once been alive, sounding his distinctive toy horn call, slamming his head against the trees, making the forest new.

Arguments over the resurrection are often presented in discrete binary categories: one believes or one doesn't; the resurrection was either literal or it was symbolic. But it seems there should be some other in-between space, a third option, existing somewhere outside the bounds of these tight frames.

Rabbi Lawrence Kushner presents a model for scriptural

interpretation that moves somewhere between, or beyond, any tidy binaries, arguing that these stories should be interpreted like dreams. With scripture, Kushner writes, "We are in possession not of the dream itself, but only of its next-morning memory. Once a dream is told, it becomes something else."

In my father's final months as a pastor, he told me about an argument he'd gotten into with a friend, about the historical accuracy of the Bible: "When it comes to the literal resurrection," my father said, "I'm still waffling on that. I go back and forth on whether Christ was literally resurrected."

I was surprised to learn that after forty-two years in the pulpit my father had not planted some stake, deciding one way or the other. This offhand comment revealed that, even for my father, there need not be an arrival at some perfect and unchanging belief. Instead, there might be only moments of rearticulation, only steps taken forward and back.

In the end, perhaps the real question is how the story changes for you, whether the resurrection was a literal, historic event or something more ambiguous; whether the resurrection refers to a singular miracle, or a story that changed and evolved over time. How does the meaning change, if Christ's resurrection foretells believers' own physical resurrection from the dead, or if this story emphasizes the necessity of transformation itself—not just of the individual, but of the collective? What changes for you, to believe that the ivory-bill is gone forever, or could be found somewhere, still?

I was thinking about these questions when I spoke with a forester, who I'll call Aaron, who worked at Cache River National Wildlife Refuge when Cornell announced that they'd found the ivory-bill nearby. Like all other federal employees I talked to about this period of time, Aaron was cagey. He'd begun talking animatedly about his experience with the ivory-bill fervor, but then his voice trailed away. "I don't actually know if I should be talking to you," he said. Maybe he needed to check with his boss first. I pleaded, and he stayed on the line. So: not his real name.

Aaron told me the ivory-bill announcement led them to change their forestry practices. Before an area was logged, they'd search to make sure there were no ivory-bills there, and they also began to implement procedures they thought might help a potential ivory-bill survive; logging fewer acres at a time, and girdling dead or undesirable trees and leaving them standing, rather than cutting them and removing them from the forest.

"Our habitat management was made even better, so after a couple years, we continued on," Aaron said. "The whole ivory-bill experience could be looked at as an embarrassment, but we looked at the evidence and we decided it was plausible. So we at least acted as if the bird was there."

This forester's emphasis on acting *as if* provided a counter to Gallagher's "big question," dividing people into camps of believers and skeptics. Rather than worrying about whether or not he *believed* in the ivory-bill's existence, this forester looked at the forest as if the bird's resurrection was possible and acted accordingly.

"Absence of evidence is not evidence of absence," the saying goes. Or, as one Arkansas biologist claimed in his guide to the Big Woods, "You can't prove that something doesn't exist." And birders still frequently patrol the Big Woods, hoping to catch a glimpse of a bird raised from the dead.

Perhaps I've felt uneasy with the language of resurrection because insisting on the resurrection of desecrated places and extinct species seems to come from desire for absolution, a desire to erase the past, and all the harm we've done, and start over with a clean slate. The truth is, forests can come back. But it takes a long, long time. Longer than three or four days locked in a cold stone tomb. Longer than the length of our lives. And so perhaps it feels impossible, a kind of magical thinking built on denial and guilt. But then I visited Craig Shackelford, a farmer in southern Arkansas.

Craig drove me out to his land, dogs panting in the backseat. The dirt and gravel road was lined on either side by cottonwoods and oaks. "You wouldn't think these trees were only twenty years old," Craig said, and he's right. The thousand acres we drove through were once a rice farm, irrigated by a ninety-acre reservoir, until Craig signed up for the Wetland Reserve Program. Two decades later, the rice fields have been replaced by shady forests, and the reservoir has become a fully-inhabited wetland, home to thousands of migrating birds each year.

I didn't know that something manmade could be so definitively wild. As Craig's truck inched along the rutted road, I glimpsed flashes of movement through the trees: birds taking off and landing or flying in great circles around the water's edge. When we parked and stepped out onto a small observation deck, the wetland swept across the horizon, as far as I could see, a riot of preening feathers and flapping wings. Above us, ibises, egrets, and herons were making their final descent, sometimes flying just a few feet over our heads, so close we could hear their wings droning, a vibrating, rhythmic hum.

"I don't know how everybody finds a bed," Craig said, chuckling. We watched the birds landing, gingerly, perching on tangles of early-growth cypress branches that formed a floating island where the birds gathered, balanced between worlds.

Most striking were the roseate spoonbills, perfectly described by the online Audubon Field Guide as "gorgeous at a distance and bizarre up close." Looking through the binoculars, I could barely make out their bright red eyes, the strange blue cast of their oblong bills and bald heads. In flight, their wings and tail feathers flashed magenta and neon pink. They show up every year around Easter, and leave by Labor Day. Craig sat in a metal chair with his dogs' leashes in

one hand and a pair of binoculars in the other. Looking out over the tumult of birds, he said, "I like rice. But I like this even more."

Wetlands like this, where the ivory-bill once lived, are themselves in-between environments, part water and part land. As massive carbon sinks, wetlands offer some of the world's best protection against the effects of climate change. The more that these habitats are destroyed, the more carbon is released in the atmosphere, and the more species we lose to extinction. The good news is that this feedback loop works in reverse too; the more swamps and bottomland forests and marshes and wetlands are protected and allowed to expand, the more carbon can be captured, the more endangered species can be protected, and the more biodiversity can be nurtured.

Looking out over the reservoir-turned-wetland, I felt buoyed by this encounter with abundance, with this place that looks nothing like diminishment at all. But many of these birds aren't supposed to be here. Roseate spoonbills typically nest much farther south, in marshes, wetlands, and mangroves along the coast. The effects of climate change—from a stronger, longer hurricane season to saltwater incursion and marsh degradation—have pushed the birds to find nesting grounds farther north. Like the ivory-bill, the roseate spoonbill was nearly extinct by the mid-twentieth century, hunted for its striking plumage. But once roseate spoonbills were placed under federal protection, their populations rebounded. And in the face of accelerating habitat loss in their traditional nesting grounds, the roseate spoonbill has so far proved resilient and adaptable.

In this place that had once been a poorly-producing rice field, it seemed irrelevant to argue about believing in resurrection, whether it really happened once long ago, whether it really might happen one day in the future. In the distance, some birds continued to arrive, landing in their nests, greeted by their downy chicks. Even though this resurrected wetland didn't result in the resurrection of the ivory-bill, the transformation from death to life was evident.

The Book of Ezekiel tells one of the most well-known stories of the resurrection of the dead. God leads the prophet Ezekiel to a valley filled with bones and asks him whether the bones might live again. Ezekiel answered, "Only you know that." But God told Ezekiel to prophesy over the bones, to command them to come to life. As Ezekiel spoke, the bones began to rattle, coming together, "bone to bone." Sinews formed between the bones, and flesh covered them, and finally breath came into these bodies and they lived again. Watching crowds of birds wading through the water, their long, curved bills skimming the matte green surface, I thought about God asking Ezekiel whether dry bones can live again, and Ezekiel's answer: *only God knows.*

As the sun lowered itself behind the cypress trees, we loaded back into Craig's truck, his dogs' hot panting breath on the back of my neck. Craig dropped me off at his hunting cabin, which was crammed, floor-to-ceiling, with taxidermied turkeys, old maps, antique pottery, and hundreds of arrowheads in glass display cases. I waved goodbye from his front porch, his truck headlights sweeping the pond's still surface as he hollered at me to check the fridge. He'd filled it with barbecued ribs, baked beans, and potato salad for my dinner.

On the wall outside the bathroom, I noticed a familiar image hanging in a wooden frame: Audubon's illustration of ivory-bills stripping bark from the trees. Craig's cabin was one of the few buildings I'd been in in Arkansas that had no religious imagery on the walls. No crosses, no Bible verses, no Jesus. In their place, this framed illustration of the Lazarus Bird seemed like its own kind of iconography.

Because Lazarus did not rise from death and ascend to heaven, some consider him resuscitated, not resurrected. To me, this only made the story more compelling. Lazarus's return to his life suggests there is salvation to be had not only in heaven but in this life, on this earth. What would that look like?

In the morning, as I drove back to the reservoir, the swamp

hibiscus blooms lining the road were opening in the relative cool of the morning. I arrived just as the sun began to rise and made coffee and oatmeal on a camp stove. In the humid haze, the birds seemed suspended somewhere between night and day, between waking and dreams.

If the universe is a parable for resurrection, as Tertullian argued, perhaps this swamp is its own kind of parable, too: In attempting to resurrect the bottomland forests of the past, we inadvertently ended up creating the habitats we would need for a strange, uncertain future. These roseate spoonbills have arrived in this fully manmade, fully wild place as harbingers—not of the past, but of our still-unfolding present. This time, in this strange land, the birds have found a place that has been prepared for them. It looked like home.

"Where there is a New Being, *there* is resurrection," Tillich wrote, "namely, the creation into eternity out of every moment in time." Through a pair of binoculars, I watched this crowd of feathered New Beings perform their morning ablutions. A white-faced ibis stood totally still with its wings outstretched and drying in the morning sun. A roseate spoonbill flapped her wings as if she were about to take flight before settling back down into her nest full of fluffy pink chicks for a few more minutes' sleep.

WOUND CARE

ON THE DAY MY son would be born, we checked into the hospital as the sun began to rise, warbling through stifling heat. That night, as I labored, each nurse who came into our room talked about the storm raging outside, which I could not hear through the hospital's thick walls.

"It's crazy out there," one nurse said, telling us about her theory that weather was making things go haywire: "We've had nine c-sections so far tonight," another nurse told me. I said I'd do anything not to be the tenth.

In the bleary days after my son was born, I struggled to name his birth. Active verbs felt wrong; after laboring for eighteen hours, doctors had cut him from my body. It didn't feel right to say I had *given birth* to him. If anything, I felt that birth had been taken from us both. In the fog of sleeplessness and Percocets, I found myself stumbling over the words, sometimes saying *my birth* instead of *his.*

And it did seem that there had been two births. In the first birth, the more straightforward one, I woke at two in the morning with contractions on the day I was scheduled to be induced. I ran a bath, turned the lights down low, and relished the feeling of each contraction as it coursed through my body. At the hospital, my son's heart rate plummeted as I pushed, and his head lodged itself in my pelvis. Just before midnight, I was wheeled into the operating room, and lifted onto the cold metal table, where strong hands pulled him from me under a cluster of blinding lights. In this birth, I can make a list of cause and effects, moving precipitously from one point on a timeline to the next.

But running parallel to that birth was another one, not contained by its parameters, veering wildly off-course. In this birth, I lose the narrative thread. In the operating room, where the anesthesiologist and my husband sat on either side of me and held down my shaking arms, my memory gets slippery. I can remember screaming that I could feel everything—the knife cutting into my skin, the awful sensation of my organs being moved around, lifted from my body. I remember the anesthesiologist saying, unhelpfully, "You should be feeling pressure, not pain." Her face was so close: smelling of fresh powder, made up into neat matte plains.

I remember Colin's voice, already fading, as he pleaded with them to fucking do something, and then the screen of my mind goes blank and black, except for one brief flash: to my left, Colin holding our baby in a striped blanket, singing "Sweet Baby James." Then nothing again, until hours later, when I'm back in a hospital room, stitched up. My son is tucked into a striped blanket, lying on my chest. The walls are moving. A nurse's voice emerges from a soundless place: "Oh," she says, "look at his eyelashes."

The next day, and the next, the nurses talked about how cool it was outside. A hurricane in the gulf had blown storms across the region, tempering the heat. "It feels like fall," one nurse said, as she gave my son his first bath. "It's like summer ended, overnight."

COVID-19 restrictions meant we could have no visitors, so we stayed in our little room, looking out the window at a world that looked the same but which everyone swore had changed.

In her essay on birth narratives, Julia Cooke begins with a quote from a doula who says that traumatic births usually have a beginning, middle, and end, a narrative arc that mirrors the traditional narrative story arc—rising tension, climax, resolution—a neat triangle, drawn in so many of my English workbooks. After the birth, I often thought that if I'd gone home and healed the way I was supposed to, the birth story I was left trying to construct would have led me to some satisfying conclusion. I would have had an emergency c-section that I did not want, and some glitch in the pain medication, and some holes in my memory, but perhaps I would've been able to reconcile that experience within a larger story of my son's birth. But if my son's birth story had a beginning and a middle, I couldn't seem to find its end.

Instead, almost as soon as we got home, I had the nagging sensation that something was wrong. Every couple of hours, I'd ask Colin to look at my incision again. He would lower himself to his knees and lightly touch the redness spreading above and below the incision's ragged line. On the fourth day, angry red streaks extended to my hip bones. My family assured me that I was probably okay, that this was probably normal, but that afternoon I shut myself into the bathroom, called the doctor who had delivered my son, and told her I was coming in.

The doctor looked at the incision and pursed her lips. She drew a dotted line with a permanent marker, tracing the edge of the redness encircling the incision, following it down around my hips. "Once you start taking antibiotics," she said, "the redness should retreat."

But the black dotted line was a permeable boundary, one that the infection promptly crossed, reddening the skin on my thighs as it spread through my bloodstream. The next morning, the doctor reopened my incision. A rush of infected fluid poured out over my belly, and she sent me to the hospital's infectious disease department. We'd left James with my parents, expecting an hour-long appointment, and would be gone for seven.

The strange cool weather that swept through during my son's birth did not stay long; once we came home, the heat returned. After a minute or two outside, his skin would turn bright red. He had no defense against the September heat. I didn't realize just how permeable he would be, apart from my body, to the world in which we both now lived.

In the hot summer months of my third trimester, my husband and I met with our doula on the porch, sitting six feet apart from each other, sweating and gulping down pitchers of water as she talked through the stages of labor. Due to the hospital's COVID-19 restrictions, our doula would not be allowed to be present in the hospital with us. For her final homework assignment, she asked me to think of an image that could serve as a guiding metaphor for birth, something I could focus on, through the pain, to give my experience of labor some trajectory, some ultimate aim.

The year 2020 did not seem like a good time to be pregnant. Maternal mortality rates rose precipitously, particularly for Black women. I knew I did not like my OB-GYN, but appointments with her were the only reason I left my house, sometimes for an entire month at a time. Our neighbor, an EMT, told us pregnant women were delaying going to the hospital for fear of contracting COVID-19: he'd answered one 911 call and found a woman standing in her front yard, holding her vernix-covered baby, umbilical cord, and placenta against her blood-stained nightgown. So I didn't change doctors. If a doctor I didn't like could get me and my son through birth alive, I thought, that would be a good enough outcome.

Besides, I was preparing in the best way I knew how: by choosing stories that could shape my son's birth, guiding us safely from beginning to end. For our doula's last assignment, I chose the James River, where Colin and I had spent so much time before we moved away from Virginia. We talked about what this guiding image signified for me. I told her about the way the river was different every time we floated our canoe down any given stretch: rain-swollen and murky in early summer, or low and clear as the summer gave way to fall. At the time, days before my son was born, I found the image of the river I loved calming and peaceful. In the aftermath of my son's birth, it seemed laughable, naive, to have harbored such high hopes.

There was one day, in the first week of my son's life, that was exactly as I imagined the early days at home with our new baby would be. I was lying on the couch in a shaft of sunlight, and my son was asleep, swaddled, next to me. Colin had strategically inserted the 1995 six-episode BBC version of *Pride and Prejudice* in the DVD player. Every time I woke up, Colin rewound the movie back to whatever scene I'd been watching when I fell asleep, so that it seemed to have no end: pastel dresses, green fields, my son's pacifier pulsing away as he slept. I thought there would be more moments of lazy respite, of snoozing during the day after sleepless nights. Instead, I fell into a deep sleep while a radiology nurse scanned my arm for blood clots. Instead, I pumped breast milk during daily antibiotic infusions, hooked up to a mass of wires. Instead, I left my days-old son with my parents while I went to the wound care clinic, where nurses hooked up IV bags of antibiotics to a needle, inserted the needle into the PICC line attached to my arm, and asked how old my son was. When I responded with five days, or nine, or twelve, they loved to tell me that the newborn days were the best days, that the newborn that I could barely hold, over the pain of my infected incision, was the sweetest part, how this stage, the stage I was missing as I spent nearly every day in the hospital, would fly right by me, was practically already over.

When you have a hole in your belly, you walk very slowly, and I often stopped in the hospital hallway to look over the directory as I made my shuffling way to the wound care clinic. The inner workings of other areas of the hospital were obscured by their names: oncology, radiology, hematology, nephrology. *Wound Care* said all you needed to know; the name itself seemed too vulnerable to say out loud, pointing too directly at the injury and the care it required.

I thought often of Leslie Jamison's essay on female pain, which I'd read years earlier, in which her boyfriend accused her of "wound-dwelling," refusing to move on from the pain of the past. Even though I couldn't bear to look directly at my wound, my whole world had been taken over by it. "A wound marks the threshold between interior and exterior," Jamison writes, "it marks where a body has been penetrated. Wounds suggest that the skin has been open—that privacy has been violated in the making of the wound, a rift in the skin, and by the act of peering into it."

And other people did peer into my wound: Rose, the wound care specialist, tiny and energetic, unwrapped the layers of tape covering my belly with intense curiosity several times a week. She measured the walls of the wound, packed it with strange strips of silver that looked like coiled fish skin, sprinkled collagen powder to help regrow tissue. Sometimes, if one side of the wound started healing too quickly, she burned it back with a Q-tip dipped in acid: a searing pain, my body tensed even as my mind tried to float away.

It's hard to describe the pain I felt, then, or to separate the layers of different kinds of pain: the strange hollow prickly sensation of the wound itself when I walked, or the tenderness of the incision under layers of tape. The ache, deep in my veins, when they inserted a hep lock and then a PICC line into my arm for antibiotic infusions. Or the totally disarming sensation of my organs still struggling, after the c-section, to find their rightful place, shifting around whenever I stood up or laid down.

In *The Body in Pain: the Making and Unmaking of the World*, Elaine Scarry describes pain's "resistance to language," which, she argues, "is not simply one of [pain's] incidental or accidental attributes but is essential to what it is." As hard as it is to describe your own pain, it's perhaps even harder to really hear the story of another person's pain, to feel it with them, unless you've been through something similar. Scarry writes that another person's pain can be neither denied or confirmed, leading pain to be cited in philosophical discourse as an example of both conviction and skepticism: "To have pain is to have certainty," she writes, "to hear of pain is to have doubt."

When I try to describe the experience of pain, of being utterly transformed by birth, I am aware that I may be speaking to—or may be heard only by—those who have experienced a similar pain, who know, through experience, what language fails to apprehend.

When I first began meeting with the therapist who specialized in traumatic births, she told me she could help with intrusive thoughts. I didn't know there was a name for what had been happening, when I woke in the night, thinking through my slim memories of the c-section, which I remembered like a production on a stage: the lights came up, and there was the blue sheet blocking my view, my arms spread wide, flashes of terror before the lights went out again. Lying in bed, I'd try to force my mind to keep the lights on, to remember a minute more, a second.

The therapist told me that she could help me make the birth into a discrete event, one that happened in the past and which had now ended. It had been over a month, but when I startled awake at night, it was not clear to me that the birth was over: I was always right back in the operating room, bumping up against the edges of my memory.

The doctor who delivered my son called and left voicemails reminding me that I needed to make an appointment for a six-week postpartum check-up. But I couldn't go back, couldn't bear to see her, to walk into that office, again. A new OB agreed to see me and requested the hospital's records of my son's birth. When I arrived at her office, two months after my son was born, she sat across from me in blue scrubs, her brown hair streaked with gray, and asked whether I had any gaps in my memory of the birth. I nodded, and she sighed, removing her glasses. She rubbed her eyes.

"They gave you ketamine," she said finally. "I think the epidural failed or had worn off, and since they couldn't do anything to numb your pain, they tried to block your memory of it. I am hoping it might help you to know that you're not going to get those memories back."

When the appointment ended, I rushed to my car to write down everything she'd said. It felt like clues to a mystery, a crime. And I did feel a surprising sense of relief, to have this question answered, to know that no amount of revisiting those gaps in my memory in the middle of the night would help fill them in any more clearly, that none of my sleepless hours would help me turn the lights back on and show me what happened between my own screams and my son's first cries.

Before I left her office, the new doctor placed my records back in the manila folder. She put her glasses back on and locked eyes with me. "If you choose to have another baby, it won't be like that," she said. "I don't know what it will be like, but it won't be like that."

In the middle of the night, I'd wake to my phone buzzing beneath my pillow every three hours, waking me to pump. I'd unplug the wound vac, which had to charge overnight, winding the long cords around my arm as quietly as I could next to James sleeping in his bassinet, and creep to the kitchen. Sometimes Colin would be up, preparing a bottle, and we'd tell each other good morning, then laugh; it was only three or four o'clock, the inky sky still hours from sunrise.

Milk clogged in painful lumps in my breasts, and every website I read suggested hot water—showers, baths—to loosen them up. But once the incision had been reopened, once the wound vac was attached to the wound under vast sheets of tape covering half of my belly, I was instructed not to bathe or shower for at least two months. Instead, I'd strip and crouch by the tub, washing myself with a wet rag. Confronting my body, I found it swollen and red, covered in bruises, dried blood, gauze, and tape, crisscrossed by wires and tubes. I did not recognize the sound of my own sobs—guttural, animal—deep, desperate moaning I'd never heard before.

I cried straight through my first few sessions with the postpartum therapist. But eventually, as I managed to piece together words to describe my son's birth, she had me assign colors to different parts of the birth. I pictured buttery yellow for the nurse who appeared in my hospital room, who had the same name as my sister, who prayed and sang while I cried; the green infused light of the hallway nurses pushed me down, on a stretcher, with my swaddled baby tucked between my knees.

As time passed after the birth, I continued assigning colors to other moments that appeared as a respite from pain: a soft, lavender purple for my mother's hands washing my hair in her kitchen sink. Cornflower blue, for quiet moments between trips to the hospital, when I held James while he slept, watching the light sweep across his face as I rocked him back and forth.

The therapist told me I could latch onto these colors when it seemed I was spiraling into a black hole. With time, I began to see these colors as the first, initial steps toward creating a narrative from what had been simply blunt, indescribable experience.

Physical pain can destroy language, causing the sufferer to revert to "pre-language cries and groans," Scarry writes. But, she writes, "to be present when a person moves up out of that pre-language and projects the facts of sentience into speech is almost to have been permitted to be present at the birth of language itself."

Because the language available to describe physical pain is so limited, Scarry writes, "two and only two metaphors" are used time and time again: the weapon and the wound.

Even though physical pain often exists without a weapon or a wound, you can imagine the kind of pain that would accompany certain kinds of weapons, and certain kinds of wounds: a split skull, a broken bone puncturing the skin. To describe their pain, a person might say the sensation was like a vice squeezing his stomach, or an ice pick in his eye, or a hammer slamming against her knee. "The point here," Scarry writes, "is not just that pain can be apprehended in the image of the weapon (or wound) but that it almost cannot be apprehended without it..."

Just as the weapon and the wound are the two metaphors chosen most often to describe a person's pain, Scarry writes that the weapon and the wound are also central to Judeo-Christian notions of God: "[T]he positioning of God and humanity at the two vertical ends of the weapon," Scarry writes, "seems to define the structure of belief itself."

Throughout the Hebrew Bible, repeated "scenes of wounding" demonstrate that "God's invisible presence is asserted, made visible" in the human body. Whether through the pains of childbirth, or in the bodies of those drowned by a God-sent flood, or turned into a pillar of salt, or covered in leprous sores, the reality of God is made visible in the wounded human body.

These wounds, Scarry writes, are often a punishment for a "failure of belief," which is the "failure to remake one's own interior in the image of God, to allow God to enter and to alter one's self...it is the refusal or inability to turn oneself inside-out, devoting one's physical interior to something outside itself, calling it by another name." A punishment and a balm, for these wounds are "explicitly presented as a 'sign' of God's realness and therefore a solution to the problem of his unreality."

❦

On the twenty-minute drive to the hospital's wound care clinic, Colin drove while I clutched my belly at the sight of a pothole or speed bump. I always cried when we walked across the yard to hand James over to my parents for our trips to the hospital, and I had no idea how we would do any of this without them—I was not supposed to be driving, we weren't allowed to bring the baby to the clinic with us, and we were still, six months into the pandemic and pre-vaccines, isolating from people outside our immediate family. I tried to imagine how we would manage my healing without my parents—not to mention Colin's health insurance, our ability to work from home, even my three unpaid months of parental leave—and came up blank.

After spending the second and third trimesters of my pregnancy in quarantine, it was jarring to find myself surrounded by people. Gloved hands guided the PICC line into place, and carefully unwrapped the gauze from my arm to attach the IV drip. At the antibiotic infusion lab, nurses asked me whether I needed to pump while receiving my infusions. If I said yes, they put me in a separate room, where I could pump in privacy while the antibiotics worked their way into my bloodstream. If I said no, I sat in the infusion lab with five or ten other people, all much older than me, and we talked. Nurses passed my phone around, cooing at pictures of my son and his shock of black hair.

At the infusion lab, I began to see that birth stories are not entirely individual, never entirely our own. They are also part of a larger, collective whole, a memory shared with all of those who have given birth before. One nurse told me stories about her children, twins, who had been born weeks early and spent more than seventy days in the neonatal intensive care unit. Since she worked in the hospital where her babies were being cared for, she went back to work immediately after their birth, spent every lunch break in their room, watching their tiny chests rise and fall as they breathed through tubes.

Once I was disconnected from the IV and allowed to leave, I'd meet my husband in the waiting room and burst into tears as I tried to relay these women's stories to him. Over time, I began to crave those hours in the infusion lab, the way the only salve for my pain was hearing about other people's pain. In my journal, I started writing a line of bell hooks's over and over: "Rarely, if ever, are any of us healed in isolation."

The other patients in the wound care clinic were mostly older, mostly diabetic, many leaning on walkers or nursing fresh amputations. As the weeks passed, the wound care specialist, Rose, grew energized by the way my body was able to heal itself. She asked me, often, if I wanted to look at the wound.

"It's closing up," she'd say. "Now's the time!" She offered to take a picture of it on my phone, for me to look at whenever I was ready. I did not take her up on it. I did not want to peer into the wound.

I often found myself walking down the long hospital hallway toward the wound care clinic with another patient. She would be a woman, decades older than me, hunched over a cane or pushing a wheelchair, and we'd both be wearing a wound vac, with tubes coiled up under our clothing, sucking out infected fluid. Or it would be a man, with a gauze sleeve covering the PICC lines implanted into his arm, just like mine.

I'd watch these other patients and think about the way Colin bent over my body each night to flush the wound with saline and dress it, carefully reattaching the wound vac, covering it in layers of tape. I'd wonder who cared for these people and their wounds, who was helping make them whole.

Years ago, writing about attending my father's church for his last year as a minister, I described my doubts as an "open wound." When I wrote that, I'd never lived with an open wound before. Now that I have, I am tempted to go back and find some other image for the pain and disorientation I felt. Implicit in this metaphor is the sense that the wound of my doubt would only be healed when I discovered steadfast belief, or renounced it altogether.

But then my (literal, not metaphorical) wound finally healed: On my birthday, I was out for a short, doctor-approved hike with Colin and James when I felt the gauze that had been packing the wound slip out from beneath the giant band-aid plastered over my incision. I laid down and removed the band-aid, as I had many times over the previous weeks, and stared up at the sky.

"Hm," Colin said, as he tried to put the gauze back in place.
"What is it?" I asked. "What's happened?"
"I think it's healed," he said. "It's closed up."

I didn't look at the incision until a few days later, after I'd gone to the wound care clinic and Rose verified that the wound had, in fact, healed. When she pronounced me graduated from treatment, it was fall, two months after my son had been born. On the way home, Colin and I stopped by a church and voted in the presidential election. I felt like I could see the world around me for the first time: piles of pumpkins for sale in a church parking lot; the leaves just beginning to change colors; the glint of light on passing cars. The wound had closed up, and the whole world had returned.

When we got home, I looked at myself in the mirror. It was the first time I'd seen the incision uncovered, totally bare. The jagged line where my body had been open was faded to almost match the color of the surrounding skin. Where the incision had been reopened, the scar was a deep divot, a healed little hole, forever offset from the rest of the incision by virtue of its separate, months-long healing process.

With the wound closed, I began to move on with my life. After the bandages and the PICC line were removed, and the wound vac was packed into its black plastic briefcase and returned to the hospital, I was allowed to take showers and go on long walks. On the other side of the wound, I began to sense the strange, singed edge of the world on which I'd been living.

In *On Being Ill*, Virginia Woolf questions why illness is not one of literature's primary themes, "[c]onsidering how common illness is, how tremendous the spiritual change that it brings, how astonishing, when the lights of health go down, the undiscovered countries that are disclosed..." With an open wound, with my "lights of health" dimmed, the world felt more tenuous and uncertain. I moved with great awareness of my body and the hole at its center, calibrating myself to the wound and its needs. And in the slow, attentive way I moved through the world, I thought often of the blank hours of birth, when I began to sense my body reaching its limits, while some other part of me remained untouched by those limits.

"[M]emories of birthing can mostly only lie," Julia Cooke writes. "With the editing of hindsight, birthing becomes a kind of self-presentation through revision." If this is true, I'm not sure, exactly, what version of myself I'm trying to present through these attempts to write a narrative of my son's birth. In my journal, the language I used to describe how I felt during and after my son's birth were words like *searing* and *flayed* and *shattered*. It took me months to admit to anyone what the birth had been for me, to say out loud to another person that it had been the most intensely spiritual experience of my life.

But just a few days after the birth, with the wound still open in my belly, I wrote in my journal that God had become "apparent" to me. So when I think about my earlier metaphor, of doubt as an open wound, it seems more accurate, now, to describe faith that way.

In *The Invisible Kingdom,* Meghan O'Rourke's account of chronic illness, she writes about doctors doubting her "testimony." I was struck by her use of a word I'd always associated with religion, with a version of Christianity I didn't grow up with personally, but recognized culturally. Testimonies—or conversion stories—have their own narrative structure. Instead of the rising action of the traditional literary narrative arc, the person giving their testimony seems only to fall deeper and deeper into the pit of sin and despair. The resolution, at the end, is uncomplicated: The storyteller hands off their own agency as they surrender to God; God's grace wipes the slate clean.

In the early days of my son's life, whenever I caught myself accidentally referring to his birth as "my birth," I felt disoriented, veering too near to the language of conversion, words like being *reborn* or *born again,* which have always made me uncomfortable, not only because they were foreign to my own religious experience, but because of my general resistance to thinking of life in terms of dramatic, decisive thresholds. Instead, our lives seem to be always changing, always altering, and we are shaped by long, mysterious arcs of transformation that come from within and without. Conversion seemed to assume that there was a static and definable point from which a person could change to another static and definable point: from fallen to saved, from doubt to belief. It all seems murkier to me than that.

But in those early days of my son's life, when I referred to the birth sometimes as his, and sometimes as my own, I seemed, in my bewilderment, to be saying something true about the conversion I was undergoing—to motherhood, and to a kind of faith—which began with birth but did not end there.

Before my son's birth, I had struggled with various conditions labeled "chronic": chronic daily headaches, chronic pain syndrome, thyroid disease, chronic nosebleeds so intense they required I have the veins inside my nostrils cauterized every few years. But none of these had been so debilitating—or so intimately coupled with my conversion to another state of being—as the wound was, both obliterating and thoroughly entwined with my experience of becoming a mother.

Now I may be verging into what O'Rourke describes as "the notion of illness as a vehicle for spiritual change," a trope in which prolonged illness imbues the sufferer with spiritual wisdom or special insight. Illness, O'Rourke writes, "is not redemptive unless it happens to be for a particular ill person." I wouldn't call my son's birth redemptive, either for my son or for myself. But it's harder, now, to know whether I'd go back and change it if I could.

Perhaps the "night side of life," as the writer Susan Sontag described illness, might be life's true side. None of us can count on a life lived in perfect health and vitality. In the end, it seems what we have in common, what might actually define our lives, are times of weakness and vulnerability, dependence, disability and frailty. Perhaps the most vulnerable version of myself is the real me: Perhaps the world seen by those dimmed lights is the real world.

In the Hebrew Bible, the human body's very capacity for woundedness speaks to the nature of the human relationship with God: "Wounding," Scarry writes, "re-enacts the power of alteration that has its first profound occurrence in creation." In the Hebrew Bible, God first makes humans, and then periodically appears on the scene to hurt us.

But in the New Testament, these "scenes of wounding" are transformed into "scenes of healing." When God becomes incarnate, taking on human form, he sets about healing wounded bodies: resurrecting the dead, healing the sick, restoring sight to the blind. Even after death, in his resurrected form, Christ's bodily wounds offer the same kind of proof of "God's realness" to his followers that they did in the Hebrew Bible. With a body, Scarry writes, God becomes "describable."

I struggle with this—perhaps because I prefer an unknowable, indescribable God, and perhaps because I struggle to believe in any final, ultimate healing for our individual or collective wounds. Perhaps my discomfort with this idea is related to my discomfort with conversion: As a convert, you become a noun, stuck in place. What resonates, for me, is a conversion that never finds its end, that never arrives anywhere fixed.

As a kid, I prided myself on my spelling abilities, but two words consistently tripped me up, then and now: *alter* and *altar*. By virtue of my confusing them for each other, these words will probably always be interchangeable and bound up in each other in my mind: change, and a place for worship—or, if not quite worship, exactly, then a place where we "turn [ourselves] inside-out," inviting the sacred to move a little closer.

In the immediate aftermath of my son's birth, it was embarrassing to remember the image I'd chosen with our doula as our guiding metaphor for birth. The peaceful river I'd imagined guiding our birth was totally discordant with the chaos and turbulence of birth itself. But in time, the river returned to me, and in hindsight seemed apt in ways I hadn't foreseen.

As soon as we shoved off from the river's edge, we were on its terms: Each stroke of our paddles in the water was a kind of hedge, announcing our intention to move forward, to veer around a boulder or over a series of rapids—an intention that was always, in the end, a kind of surrender, a compromise. On rare occasions, our boat capsized in rough water; we often hit rocks we fully expected to pass by. Our journeys down the James River had never proceeded from beginning to end: Wherever we launched our boat was not the beginning, and wherever we climbed out at the end of the day was not the end. We began mid-stream and we ended that way, too.

In *Meander, Spiral, Explode: Design and Pattern in Narrative*, the writer Jane Alison explores alternatives to the traditional narrative arc structure. "A radial narrative," she writes, "could spring from a central hole—an incident, pain, absence, horror—around which it keeps circling or from which it keeps veering, but it scarcely moves forward in time."

The poet Fanny Howe writes about pursuing bewilderment "as a poetics and a politics." In a maze, a spiral, or a labyrinth, she writes, there is "no plain path, no up and down, no inside or outside. But there are strange returns and recognitions and never a conclusion."

Bewilderment, Howe writes, "begins to form, for me, more than an attitude—but an actual approach—a way—to settle with the unresolvable." Bewilderment "shows not only how to get lost but also how it feels not to return."

⁂

One of my friends who was raised in conservative, charismatic churches likes to argue with me about the liberal Protestant penchant for metaphors and symbolic interpretations. "It just seems to me that something has to be literally true," he said one day over the phone. "It can't all be just a metaphor."

I was out on a walk when he called and it had started to drizzle. I stood out of the rain under a neighbor's large cypress tree, the phone pressed to my ear. "But I don't think of metaphors as *just*," I said, something I didn't know I believed until I said it.

If metaphors are how we can most effectively describe our pain to each other, and if metaphors are how we can most clearly describe God or articulate the presence of an ineffable *something* that so many of us apprehend, then it seems to me that metaphors might be as close as we can get to the thing itself: to healing, to what is holy.

That day, my friend and I had been talking about the story, from Exodus, of the burning bush. I was telling him about a translation I'd recently encountered. When Moses asks to know God's name, the name God gives Moses, in Hebrew, is *Ehyeh Asher Ehyeh*. In most versions of the Bible that I grew up with, this is translated as "I am who I am," or "I am that I am." But this translation doesn't really hold up to scrutiny.

Rabbi Lawrence Kushner writes that Biblical Hebrew has "only two tenses, usually called past and future, but more precisely perfect and imperfect." These tenses describe actions as either complete or incomplete. By answering *Ehyeh Asher Ehyeh*, Kushner writes, God uses "not the 'present' and static 'I am that I am,' or even the dynamic 'I will be who I will be,' but the yet imperfect, 'I am not yet who I am not yet.' God in effect says, 'I am still Myself, becoming.'"

If the story of the burning bush is a metaphor—and I believe it is—it might reveal that God is found not in the healing of the bush, or in the restoration of the bush to its pre-burned state. Instead, God is embodied by a fire that burns without ceasing (a weapon), but also without consuming (an impossible wound).

"Metaphor is a talking cure," the writer Catherine Madsen writes, "it starts at the point of injury." If all we have, in the end, are metaphors—our attempts at self-cure—we are left with a story in which our experience of God shifts from wounding to healing, from inflicting pain on us to embodied suffering alongside us.

Which I take to mean, as Octavia Butler wrote, that "God is change." Or Teresa of Ávila: "The feeling remains that God is on the journey, too." That, if nothing else, God is with us in our bewilderment.

My son was almost two years old when I began seeing a physical therapist for severe back pain. The pain would start somewhere deep in my pelvis and radiate unpredictably, ricocheting through my back, throbbing in my sacrum, shooting down one leg and then the other. Anything could trigger the pain: doing yoga or not doing yoga; walking or not walking; loading the dishwasher, lifting my son from his crib, or sitting still for hours in fear of the pain.

By this time, we seemed far from birth. Whenever I told James I was going to the grocery store, he'd ask for ice cream; at night, after I put him in bed and turned off the light, I'd hear him blowing kisses at me in the dark; every morning, when I asked him what he dreamed about overnight, he'd say puppies. I did not think for a moment that the pain was related to birth—which had, of course, surely, found an end long ago.

But then the physical therapist asked me to stand in front of her with my arms at my sides as she walked a slow circle around me. "Your ribs are still flared from pregnancy," she said. "Your breath is disconnected from your diaphragm. Your hips are turned outward in a birthing position."

She had me lie face-down on her table, and she pressed her hands into either side of my pelvis, pushing inward as if she could manually reshape my skeleton. She was quiet for a long time, and then she whispered words for me to repeat: "I am no longer pregnant. My delivery is complete." It felt like an entirely new story, something my body had yet to hear.

"What gives a spiraling narrative a sense of ending?" Alison writes. "Good question, for spirals could go on forever."

When I first met with the therapist who specialized in traumatic births, she told me she could help me make meaning out of my experience of my son's birth. I wrote the word "meaning" in my journal and circled it, like it was an entirely new concept. My son was only a month old. I hadn't yet learned about the ketamine; I was still trying to fill in the gaps in my memory. The idea that my son's birth could cohere into a story that not only had a beginning, middle, and end, but a meaning, seemed like a stretch.

I kept thinking that if the incision had healed and not been reopened—if the incision had become a scar, instead of a wound—perhaps my sense of the story of my son's birth would have ended there. Perhaps, I calculated, if things had gone even slightly differently, I would not continue circling the night of my son's birth and the weeks that followed, trying to pry apart even one event from another in order to plot them, get things in order, and find the end.

Something changed when the postpartum therapist asked me how the story of my son's birth might shift if I considered a change in the audience: "What would you tell your son about his birth?"

If the story of your birth had been a tangled ball of yarn, in that moment it came undone, and I was left holding a single strand: "I'd tell him how much we loved him," I said. "How excited we were that he was finally here."

The year before you were born, we had just begun thinking of having a child. We were in Virginia, the place where we'd met, driving along the wide, winding James River. We agreed that if we had a baby boy, we would name him after the river we'd loved so well during our first years together. By the next week, I was pregnant.

If the story of your birth had been a labyrinth, when the spiral suddenly straightened, I followed that wide, clear path out of the story and into our lives.

"We spoke you into existence," we told you, often, in your earliest days. "We said your name and you appeared."

NOTES AND FURTHER READING

THE CHARGED WORLD

Li-Young Lee, from *A God in the House: Poets Talk About Faith* edited by Ilya Kaminsky and Katherine Towler

Thomas Merton, *No Man is an Island*

WORLD WITHOUT END

Marcus Borg, *Speaking Christian: Why Christian Words Have Lost Their Meaning and Power–And How They Can Be Restored*

Elizabeth Rush, "The Marsh at the End of the World," *Guernica Magazine*

Robin Globus Veldman, *The Gospel of Climate Skepticism*

Matthew Avery Sutton, *American Apocalypse: A History of Modern Evangelicalism*

THE ARK AT THE END OF THE WORLD

Randall Balmer, *The Making of Evangelicalism*

Randall J. Stephens and Karl W. Giberson, *The Anointed: Evangelical Truth in a Secular Age*

Meghan O'Gieblyn, *Interior States*
Peter Kropotkin, *Mutual Aid: A Factor of Evolution*
Cole Arthur Riley, *This Here Flesh: Spirituality, Liberation, and the Stories that Make Us*
Wil Gafney—*Between Babel and Babble: Pentecost*—The Rev. Wil Gafney, Ph.D. Womanists Wading in the Word™

CRYING IN CHURCH

Wendell Berry, "The Contrariness of the Mad Farmer"

TV APOCALYPSE

Mark O'Connell, *Notes from an Apocalypse*
Instagram account—Jericho Vincent, @thealef
Podcast—"How to Survive the End of the World," adrienne maree brown and Autumn Brown

THIS IS PARADISE

Jordan Kisner, *Thin Places: Essays from In Between*
Emma Marris, *Rambunctious Garden*
Adrian Shirk, *Heaven is a Place on Earth: Searching for an American Utopia*
Abraham Joshua Heschel, *Moral Grandeur and Spiritual Audacity*

THE TERMINAL SEA

Lawrence Kushner, *The River of Light: Spirituality, Judaism, Consciousness*
Erik Reece, *Utopia Drive: A Road Trip Through America's Most Radical Idea*

FOR THE LIVING OF THESE DAYS

Rachel Held Evans, *Evolving in Monkey Town* (since re-titled *Faith Unraveled*)
Danté Stewart, *Shoutin' in the Fire: An American Epistle*

Kristin Kobes Du Mez, *Jesus and John Wayne: How White Evangelicals Corrupted a Faith and Fractured a Nation*

Imani Perry, *South to America: A Journey Below the Mason-Dixon to Understand the Soul of a Nation*

NATURAL ENDS

Suzanne Kelly, *Greening Death*

Lee Webster (editor), *Changing Landscapes: Exploring the growth of ethical, compassionate, and environmentally sustainable green funeral practices*

THE LIFE EVERLASTING

Tim Gallagher, *The Grail Bird: The Rediscovery of the Ivory-billed Woodpecker*

Paul Tillich, *The New Being*

E.O. Wilson, *A Window on Eternity: A Biologist's Walk Through Gorongosa National Park*

Kevin J. Madigan and Jon. D. Levenson, *Resurrection: The Power of God for Christians and Jews*

Elaine Pagels, *The Gnostic Gospels*

Elaine Pagels, *Beyond Belief: the Secret Gospel of Thomas*

Helen Macdonald, *Vesper Flights*

WOUND CARE

Leslie Jamison, *The Empathy Exams*

Elaine Scarry, *The Body in Pain: the Making and Unmaking of the World*

Virginia Woolf, *On Being Ill*

Meghan O'Rourke, *The Invisible Kingdom*

Susan Sontag, *Illness as Metaphor*

Jane Alison, *Meander, Spiral, Explode: Design and Pattern in Narrative*

Fanny Howe, *The Wedding Dress*

Octavia Butler, *Parable of the Sower*

Catherine Madsen, "Notes on God's Violence," *CrossCurrents*

ACKNOWLEDGMENTS

Thank you to everyone who allowed me into their lives for this book, who opened their homes, gave me their time, and answered questions I often wasn't sure how to ask.

Thanks to my parents, Don Park and Sherry Lear-Park, for raising me in a world of faith that I could live and grow with. Thank you for being interested in all my questions—and for living those questions alongside me. Thank you for encouraging me as a mother and writer, for being our next door neighbors, and for being Mimi and Pop to our children.

To Courtney and Alan: thank you for holding down the Compound's eastern quadrant. We are grateful to be your neighbors.

Deep gratitude to Denny and Joetta Lee, for many Camp Nana Papas, and for the selflessness and care that you unfailingly offer to the most vulnerable—and to us and our children.

Thank you to the childcare workers who have supported our family and my creative life by caring for our children. Thank you to my companions in motherhood, especially Gal Flam and Shelley

Johnson. Thank you to my extended family, including Lee, Mary Leslie, Joni, Billy, and David.

Thank you to Samantha Shea for helping me find my way to this book, and thank you to Katherine Webb, Meg Reid, Kate McMullen, Julie Jarema, and everyone at Hub City for bringing it to life.

For companionship and conversations, thank you to Nathan Brasfield, Eileen Townsend, and Daniel Williford. Thank you to the spiritual wisdom and buoyant joy of Chaplain Jon Powers.

Thanks to the House of Peace and Justice, Hollins University, the Virginia Center for the Creative Arts, Penland School of Crafts, the Religion and Environment Story Project, Sumanth Prabhaker, Josina Guess, Meera Subramanian, and Stephen Prothero.

Thank you to the publications where these essays first appeared, often in very different form: *Orion Magazine, Guernica, The Bitter Southerner, Image Journal,* and *The Louisville Review.*

To Chet'la Sebree, Lena Moses-Schmitt, Grant Kittrell, Amy Butcher, Joe Manning, and Austyn Gaffney: gratitude for the art you make and the worlds you envision and create. Thank you for traveling alongside me.

Exuberant thanks to Carrie Brown, for your friendship and generous spirit.

To the memory of my grandmother, Nellie Marie Park, my first great love.

To Colin Lee, for everything, my whole life, all of it. Thank you for your belief.

To James River Lee and Juniper Marie Lee: our bright lights.

The COLD MOUNTAIN *Fund*

SERIES

NATIONAL BOOK AWARD WINNER Charles Frazier generously supports publication of a series of Hub City Press books through the Cold Mountain Fund at the Community Foundation of Western North Carolina. The Cold Mountain Series spotlights works of fiction by new and extraordinary writers from the American South. Books published in this series have been reviewed in outlets like the the Boston Globe, Wall Street Journal, San Francisco Chronicle, Garden & Gun, People Magazine, and Entertainment Weekly; included on Best Books lists from NPR, Kirkus Reviews, and the American Library Association; and have won or been nominated for awards like the Southern Book Prize, the Ohioana Book Award, Crooks Corner Book Prize, and the Langum Prize for Historical Fiction.

PREVIOUS TITLES

Beautiful Dreamers • Minrose Gwin

Good Women • Halle Hill

The Say So • Julia Franks

The Crocodile Bride • Ashleigh Bell Pedersen

Child in the Valley • Gordy Sauer

The Parted Earth • Anjali Enjeti

You Want More: The Selected Stories of George Singleton

The Prettiest Star • Carter Sickels

Watershed • Mark Barr

The Magnetic Girl • Jessica Handler

HUB CITY PRESS books are made possible through the generous support of grants and donations from corporations, state and federal grant programs, family foundations, and the many individuals who support our mission of building a more inclusive literary arts culture, in particular: Byron Morris and Deborah McAbee, Charles and Katherine Frazier, and Michel and Eliot Stone. Hub City Press gratefully acknowledges support from the National Endowment for the Arts, the Amazon Literary Partnership, the South Carolina Arts Commission, Spartanburg County Public Library, and the City of Spartanburg.